Acknowledgements

GW00384664

SSADM was developed for the Central Computer and Telecommunications Agency (CCTA) in 1980. It is the standard method for IT projects in Central Government, and is believed to be the most widely-used method in the UK private sector. The National Computing Centre Limited (NCC) and the CCTA collaborate on the development, support and promotion of SSADM. I should like to acknowledge permission from the CCTA to include the *Reference Manual Stage Diagrams* in Chapters 12-18.

I would particularly like to acknowledge with thanks the following people, for their help in reviewing the draft in the midst of their many other commitments. Their comments on the material have been of great help to me.

P J Crompton	Heywood & Partners Limited
Dr G R Hudson	Handforth Health Centre
Michael McCann	Rede Group
Dr Ian Procter	Omnis IT Consultants Limited
Brian West	The National Computing Centre Limited
Chris Williams	Kingsley Enterprises

Preface

SSADM, the Structured Systems Analysis and Design Method, has been in existence since 1980. It is a method to help systems analysts and designers with their work. The method has been kept under review since its inception, to keep abreast of developments in methods and techniques, and to take into account the experience and comments of its many users. The method has now advanced to Version 4, which is the version described here.

This book updates *Introducing SSADM Version 3* and also draws on material previously published in the *SSADM Developer's Handbook* and *Getting the System You Want: A User's Guide to SSADM* all published by The National Computing Centre Limited. The book is in four parts.

Part 1 explains why it is necessary to use a method for systems analysis and design, and how SSADM meets these needs; a general overview is given of SSADM. The critical importance of setting objectives for the system is then discussed, as it is by ensuring through quality assurance that objectives are met.

Finally in this part, the elements of a system are considered to discover the information that must be established during systems analysis. Then what is done in SSADM will be seen to follow a logical and necessary pattern.

Part 2 looks at the principal techniques used in SSADM and how they relate to the essential elements of systems. After an introduction about the diagrammatic approach, the three main diagramming techniques of Data Flow Modelling, Logical Data Modelling and Entity-Event Modelling are introduced. These techniques complement each other to give a three-dimensional view of a system. This part is completed by a chapter on the Requirements Catalogue.

Part 3 is devoted to the activities carried out in SSADM; described as stages, steps and tasks. This is the framework that the investigation follows, and on which the facts are hung as they are found. SSADM can be regarded as prescriptive guidelines: prescriptive in that it sets out all the things that should be considered, and guidelines in that it does require the employment of common sense and sound management, rather than blind faith.

Part 4 introduces management implications. Whilst SSADM provides the tools and the approach that aid the development of effective systems, it doesn't stop people from making mistakes and losing control. Quality assurance and project management are also required, and are catered for within the method. Practical aspects are considered, including the use of CASE tools and suggestions as to the way in which the method can be introduced into an organisation

Introducing SSADM Version 4 is one of a series of books produced by NCC/Blackwell in support of SSADM.

Version 3 is supported by:

- *SSADM Manual.*

- *Introducing SSADM.*

- *SSADM Developer's Handbook.*

- *Getting the System You Want — A User's Guide to SSADM.*

Version 4 is supported by:

- *SSADM Version 4 Manual.*

- *A User's Guide to SSADM:* currently being prepared.

Furthermore, it is anticipated that a series of Subject Guides will be produced to enhance the use of SSADM in various specialised circumstances, and also within a diversity of software development environments.

Contents

           Introduction   65
           Drawing comparisons   65

11   The Requirements Catalogue   69

           Introduction   69
           Allocating priorities   70
           Precision in requirements   70
           Specifying requirements in a measurable way   71
           Principal uses of the requirements catalogue
              within SSADM   71

PART 3: SSADM Activities

Requirements Analysis Module

12   Stage 0 – Feasibility   75

           Introduction   75

           Step 010   Prepare for the Feasibility Study   75
           Step 020   Define the problem   78
           Step 030   Select Feasibility Options   78
           Step 040   Assemble Feasibility Report   79

13   Stage 1 – Investigation of Current Environment   81

           Introduction   81

           Step 110   Establish analysis framework   81
           Step 120   Investigate and define requirements 84
           Step 130   Investigate current processing   84
           Step 140   Investigate current data   85
           Step 150   Derive logical view of current services 85
           Step 160   Assemble investigation results   86

14   Stage 2 – Business System Options   87

           Introduction   87

           Step 210   Define Business System Options   87
           Step 220   Select Business System Option   87

Requirements Specification Module

Logical System Specification Module

Physical Design Module

PART 4: Implementing SSADM – Considerations for Management

1
Introduction

System development is not easy. One of the best descriptions of the task was given by Lawrence J Peters, in a thought-provoking consideration of the subject (*Peters, 1981*). He put into words what many developers had, to their cost, found but not defined or perhaps even realised before. Among Peters' conclusions were:

- the solution of any difficulty can reveal even more serious difficulties;

- specifications are never complete: there is always something more that could be added;

- there is no single, correct solution to a problem: there is always the possibility that a better solution could be found given more time;

- there are no right or wrong solutions: only good or bad ones;

- neither the number of possible solutions nor the means of obtaining them is limited.

It must be accepted that perfection, in the shape of a system that will do everything that everyone wants, that never fails, and never needs to be changed, is impossible. What *is* possible is to build effective systems that can achieve those objectives that have been precisely specified. This can be done given three provisos:

- A computer department that is technically competent and capable of delivering good systems - SSADM is an aid to competence.

- End users who are actively involved in the development process and who make the business decisions — SSADM requires this.

- The documentation produced by the developers is understandable to the end users — and a prodigiously thick English narrative specification is rarely understandable and is also usually ambiguous. If there is any

1

ambiguity, it is a safe bet that some people will read it one way and that others, during the further development of the system, will read it differently. SSADM avoids this with documentation that, being diagrammatic, is neither ambiguous nor difficult to understand.

The 'Them and Us' situation is regrettably common in many aspects of human relationships − Catholics and Protestants, East and West, home and away teams, men and women, management and unions and, in computer terms, users and developers. In other words there are two sides, and when anything goes wrong, each blames the other. "You never *told* me that," says the analyst. "You never *asked* me that," responds the user.

SSADM gives the opportunity to get away from all that. Development becomes a team effort involving management, users and practitioners. Without this involvement, development is likely to get out of control and systems are likely to do what the developers thought was needed, rather than what the users actually require. (Software houses, developing general systems for sale to many users, are in a different position. From their research and experience they must anticipate the requirements of their intended market).

It is a responsibility of corporate management to ensure that:

  − the systems being developed are the right ones for the company;

  − the expense and time involved are justifiable and will help the company to meet its objectives;

  − the development is proceeding according to plan.

It is a responsibility of user management to ensure that both they and their staff:

  − co-operate with the developers in preparing a project plan;

  − agree the user content of the plan;

  − know what is expected of them during development;

  − commit adequate resources to the project.

It is a responsibility of systems development management to ensure that technical resources with the necessary levels of:

  − SSADM expertise;

  − business experience;

  − project management skills;

are all available as and when required, and that any divergence from the plan has been accepted by management before it is implemented.

The remaining chapters in Part 1 aim to provide a basic understanding of the method so that organisations considering taking it on will appreciate what the method has to offer, will have some idea of the implications if they do, and stand the best chance of making a success of it, if they follow the practical suggestions outlined in Chapter 23.

2
Why a method is necessary

The first commercial data processing system went live in 1954 (payroll on a LEO computer). Yet, after more than 35 years of data processing, system developments still often tend to be more of an art than a science; to be more closely related to anarchy than to discipline. Developments commonly overrun budgets on both time and cost, and fail to produce systems that meet the real needs of their users.

A survey (*PA Computers and Telecommunications, 1985*) showed that of the projects covered by their study:

- 66 percent stated a timescale overrun;

- 55 percent stated that effort was over budget;

- 58 percent were affected by a major unexpected problem.

Anyone reading the computer press will see reports almost every week of major projects that have gone off the rails. Things don't appear to have improved a great deal since 1985. Clearly a betting man would get good odds against work being completed to schedule. It is instructive to consider what happens if a method is not used for system development. Without a method, every project is developed in a different way. (Projects developed in the same way each time *are* using a method.) The chances are that, without a method, the system is likely to be late, will probably cost more than was expected, and may well not do what the user expects or wants.

If systems are never developed in the same way twice, then there is no bank of expertise on which to draw – so there are major management and technical problems with:

- *Estimates.* Without comparable past experience, there is no firm foundation on which future estimates can be based. There are very severe problems in attempting to work to an over-optimistic estimate, particularly for anyone working to a fixed price contract. If the system is

5

delivered on time, in these circumstances, then corners have probably been cut, often on testing, and such systems tend to be unreliable.

- *Control.* Control is notoriously inaccurate when based on estimates of how long it will take to finish a task. (Development staff are notoriously over-optimistic.) Effective control is only possible from the existence of completed work in the form of documentation *end products*) produced at the end of each task. The project manager must be able to establish the precise stage that the project has reached (by end products completed), and how far there is still to go (by tasks remaining).

- *Completeness.* Without some sort of checklist of activities, people cannot be sure that they have remembered to do everything. Anything that is missed or not done in the best sequence is going to cost more later on. The developers must try to do things at the best time. Pay now, or pay more later.

In the absence of a method, what exists is an uncontrollable, incomplete, free-for-all. Ad hoc approaches to development have a long history of not producing the goods. It is not the way to go about developing systems. As the free-for-all peters out, those involved in the project come to their final task − that of apportioning blame. A high staff turnover helps. Then the blame can be attributed to someone who has left.

Over the years a number of techniques has been found to improve specific areas of system development. The integration of techniques in a prescribed way constitutes a development method. Standardising on a method permits developments to be done in the same way each time, and thus provides a basis for estimation, management, control, and subsequent maintenance.

The *1987 NCC Members Survey* indicated that software development methods were used by only 32 percent of those who responded, and they tended to be the big organisations employing in excess of 10,000 people. Yet clearly the use of methods was worthwhile. Among the percentage improvements reported were:

- quality of product   33 percent;

- productivity of staff   22 percent;

- timeliness of delivery   17 percent;

- system life cycle costs   28 percent.

Perhaps yours is a much smaller business. Will the method work in your organisation? The answer is an unqualified YES. It is difficult to envisage any system that would take more than a handful of man days to develop, that would not benefit from the *intelligent* application of SSADM.

Successful organisations and staff are constantly striving to improve their performance. The question for them to ask should not be "Should our organisation be using a method?" but rather:

> **Can it afford not**
>
> **to use a method?**

Part 1

Introduction

3

What SSADM has to offer

INTRODUCTION

In claiming a method as being the best, the question must arise, "Best for what?" No one method could hope to be perfect for every:

- type of system development;

- level of complexity;

- size of installation;

- level of experience;

- size of team;

- cost and time constraints;

- language or development environment in which a system may be implemented.

With literally hundreds of methods, techniques and approaches from which to choose, and with existing methods themselves undergoing constant development, it would be rash indeed to claim SSADM as the best. What can be claimed for SSADM is that it is a good, well tried method, and that it works well in the area of development at which it is aimed — the analysis and design of commercial data processing and information systems.

However, SSADM does have many attributes. It is worth recounting reasons why it was chosen by, and developed with, the Central Computer and Telecommunications Agency (CCTA), and subsequently chosen as the method to be supported by The National Computing Centre. Many of these considerations will also apply within your own organisation.

HISTORY

Civil Service computing departments, in common with many in the private sector, suffer from a high staff turnover and the consequent lack of a sufficient number of experienced people. They required a way of working that would enable inexperienced people to make an effective contribution quickly, and this was seen as being a method that:

- was already in existence (1980) and close to being what they wanted;

- could be taught easily;

- would dovetail with their standard method of program design; essentially Jackson Structured Programming, or JSP (*Jackson 1975, Ingevaldsson 1980*);

- would dovetail with project control;

- was capable of support by software tools.

The UK government department with overall responsibility for information technology in the civil service is the *Central Computer and Telecommunications Agency (CCTA)*. Many methods were considered by the CCTA, who eventually chose the one which, after further development, became SSADM.

In 1984, as part of a study sponsored by the Commission of the European Communities and the United Kingdom Government, NCC undertook to establish the ideal attributes for a method and then to review some of those which were then currently available, to see how they matched this 'ideal'. Meanwhile, work on developing a method elsewhere within NCC was temporarily suspended.

The investigation in due course resulted in the derivation of a checklist of 44 attributes against which methods could be compared. SSADM was found to be a very close match to the 'ideal', and was also remarkably similar to the development within NCC. In view of the existing user base for SSADM (almost all UK government computing) it was decided that NCC should collaborate with the CCTA in promoting the use of SSADM in the private sector.

ATTRIBUTES

The benefits of SSADM come not only from the engineering rigour of a method but also, and perhaps even more importantly, from the fact that it offers protection of company investment in systems and in people, and a broad base of supply and support. Its attributes can be summarised into the following categories.

Theoretical:

- it closely matches the carefully researched 'ideal';

- it contains the generally accepted best current techniques.

The method itself:

- SSADM is tried and tested, is widely used, and it works;

- it is well documented, with documentation that is publicly available;

- it is a stable product that will only change in a controlled and considered way in the light of experience, and of new technological developments;

- it provides a national, non-proprietary, *de facto* standard;

- users will not be locked-in to a single supplier − training and consultancy are available from many organisations;

- software support for the method is available, again from many organisations.

The system:

- three independent but cross-checking viewpoints ensure that the delivered system will be closer to the ultimate one, ie there will be fewer of the inadvertent omissions that would otherwise turn up as enhancements during maintenance;

- the emphasis on data held produces a sound, flexible design;

- the system will be described in an unambiguous specification;

- easier and better validation can be carried out on the analysis and design;

- early identification is given of possible problems;

- a logical design is produced that is independent of equipment (hardware) and implementation language (software); this design can then be implemented (given its physical form) within any computing environment.

Project management and control:

- the structural framework of the method helps in planning, defining what tasks should be carried out, and when they should be done;

- the standard approach permits collection of statistics and therefore better future estimates based on actual experience in the installation.

- completed products compared with the checklist of tasks show how much has been done, and what work still remains;

- end products of each step permit project control by actual achievements rather than by estimates of progress.

Technical staff:

- SSADM makes effective use of both experienced and inexperienced people;

- communication between team members is more effective;

- the team is more resilient to the loss cf key staff;

- because of the stability of the method, the cost of training represents an investment rather than an expense;

- new staff are quite likely to know the method.

Users:

- users are closely involved with the work right from the start, and their contribution is critical to the success of the project;

- better communication between users and developers causes fewer misunderstandings and consequent rework.

Contractors:

- The method provides known standards for them to work to;

- SSADM is likely to be known to them already.

Maintenance

There are significant savings on maintenance:

- thorough analysis ensures that from the start there are fewer accidental omissions and logic errors;

- integral documentation, created throughout development, gives a thorough, detailed picture of the system, which aids understanding and helps to make clear the consequences of proposed changes;

- more effective use of resources is achieved during maintenance itself because the systems are well structured, both for data and processes, and so changes are easier to implement.

4

An outline of SSADM

INTRODUCTION

The development of computer systems entails many activities. Together, these activities are known as phases in the system life cycle. The life cycle can be drawn in many ways in an attempt to show what really happens during system development.

Figure 4.1 is the simplest version of a life cycle and shows nothing of the iterative nature of the work that takes place within and between phases. Its only purpose is to indicate where SSADM fits within the total of all the development activities.

Systems analysis and design are critically important phases of the systems development process. Errors and omissions during these phases, that are not discovered until after coding or later, can be much more costly to resolve than if they were picked up shortly after they were made. (Some surveys have shown that the cost can be 100 times as high.)

SSADM is a formalised method that addresses much of this critical work. It consists of:

- *Tasks,* ie *what* is to be done, and *when* it should be done. (Whilst SSADM sets out the tasks to be considered, these are in the nature of guidelines rather than a strict set of rules that must be followed blindly in all circumstances.);

- *Techniques,* ie *how* the work is to be done;

- *Documents,* ie *where* the information gathered about the system is to be recorded. (Some of these may be replaced by software that assists with the application of the method. Such software is known as CASE (Computer Aided Software Engineering).

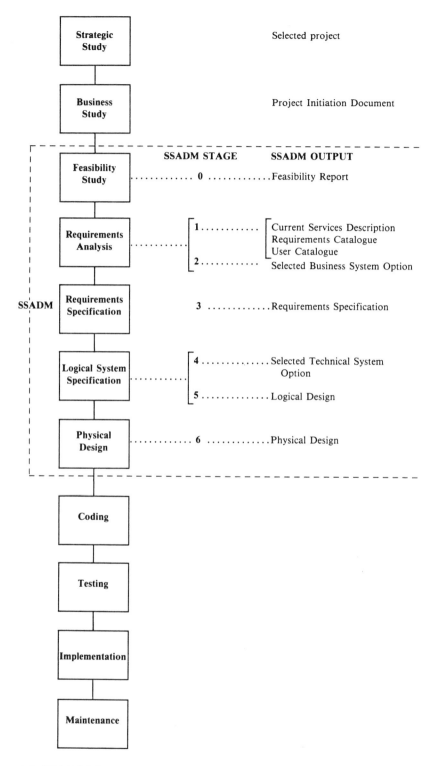

Figure 4.1 SSADM in a system development life cycle

Other software that may be used with the method includes: data dictionaries, word processors, and spreadsheets. (Software is also available to help with project management.)

SSADM, whilst complementing other development activities, does not encompass them all. For instance, it does not itself cover what may be regarded as the basic skills of the analyst, which include such tasks as interviewing, writing reports, making presentations, forms design, and screen design. The interfaces of SSADM with other aspects of development are shown in Figure 4.2.

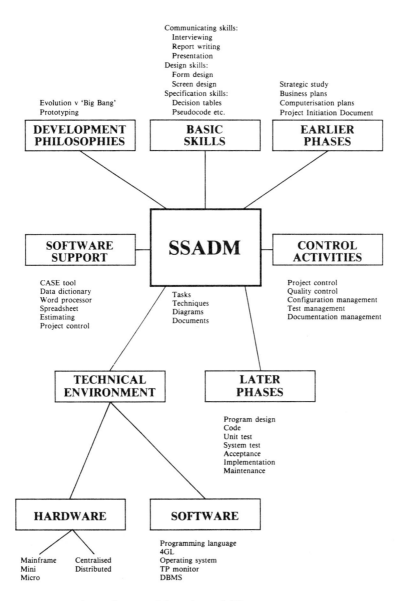

Figure 4.2 SSADM interfaces with other skills

Looking at SSADM a little more closely, Figure 4.3 shows what goes into SSADM, what it consists of, and what the final products are.

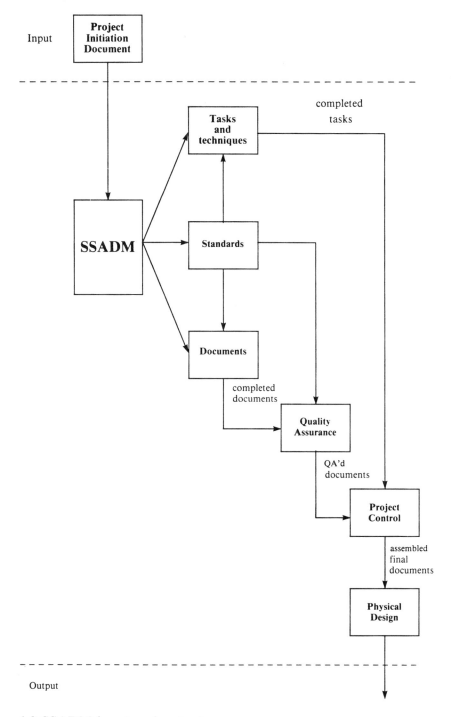

Figure 4.3 SSADM input and output

The *Project Initiation Document* gives the input to SSADM as provided by management. It gives the first definition of the area of study, and the aims and objectives of the system. It is known by many other names, depending on the organisation. Some of these are:

- Analysis Requirement;

- Analysis Startup Document;

- Terms of Reference;

- User Requirement.

Standards are the way in which the work is carried out, ie the correct application of the tasks, techniques and completion of documents as specified in SSADM, and perhaps modified within the installation.

Quality Assurance is the formal checking that the work has been carried out thoroughly and correctly. This is done by ensuring that all the documents that should have been produced are, in fact, present and that they have been completed to the required standard.

Project Control is management of the project. This is done by monitoring completion of tasks, proved by the availability of completed documents, estimating the remaining workload, and allocating resources accordingly.

Physical Design is the collection of documents which fully define the system that is required.

The output documents all go forward to later phases in the development life cycle.

Figure 4.4 shows the general structure of SSADM.

STAGE DIAGRAMS

The stage diagrams, featured in Chapters 12-18, are abridged only slightly from those in the SSADM Manual. They may appear confusing at first sight but are not difficult to follow once the principles are known. The general layout is shown in Figure 4.5.

Plan, Monitor and Control

Project procedures such as planning, estimating, and quality reviews are not a part of SSADM activities, but interface with them. The interface is the *Information Highway*. SSADM products and reports are shown as going from the activities to the Highway. To simplify the diagrams, the *Plan, Monitor* and *Control* box has been omitted from the diagrams, but is implicit on all of them.

SSADM consists of

5 modules:
— Feasibility Study
— Requirements Analysis
— Requirements Specification
— Logical System Specification
— Physical Design

The modules are broken down into 7 stages:
— 1 in Feasibility Study
— 2 in Requirements Analysis
— 1 in Requirements Specification
— 2 in Logical System Specification
— 1 in Physical Design

Each of the 7 stages is broken down into steps.
There are 33 steps in all.

Each step is further sub-divided into tasks, of
which there are 149 in all.

Each task has an end product

The end products are subject to a Quality
Assurance (QA) Review

Project control is done by checking that all
work on the specified end products, both
development and QA, has been completed.

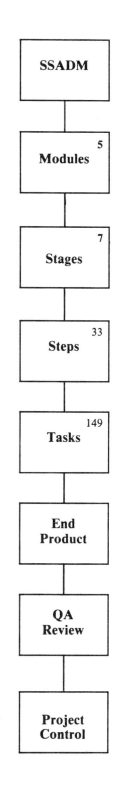

Figure 4.4 The general structure of SSADM

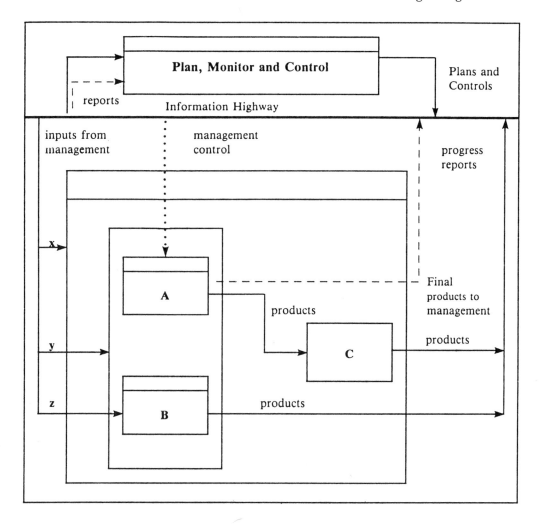

Figure 4.5 The SSADM stage diagrams

Information Highway

The Information Highway marks the division between the technical and the management processes. Flows of products between activities on the same diagram are drawn directly, but products and reports that pass between technical processes via a management activity are shown as being connected to the Highway. Thus all products going from one stage to the next go via the Highway as they progress via a quality review.

Inputs from management

Inputs from management are shown as coming from the Information Highway to the edge of a box. They are available to all the processes bounded by the box. Thus items shown as x are available to all three Steps A, B and C. Items noted y are available to Steps A and B. Items at z are available only to Step B.

Management controls and authorisation

Aspects of the development which are controlled by management are shown by dotted lines coming down from the Information Highway.

Progress reports

Progress reports are indicated by dashed lines from the processes to the Information Highway.

Parallel steps

Steps which are done in parallel are shown enclosed in the same box. Thus in Figure 4.5, Steps A and B are done in parallel.

5

The elements of a system

INTRODUCTION

Before looking at what happens within SSADM, it is as well to have an understanding of what the application of SSADM is trying to achieve. This chapter therefore ignores computers and considers instead the nature of systems. The aim is to establish what facts the analysts must discover before they can properly specify a system.

Imagine a purely manual system, with no part of it automated in any way. There may be no written instructions – what needs doing may be held in people's heads. When the lights are switched off at night and everyone goes home, all that is left behind is a heap of data – in filing cabinets, on record cards, on notes and memos. The critical base of the system is:

DATA

The next morning the office is opened up, people come in, and things start to happen: the telephone rings; the mail arrives; people visit; payment of an invoice is authorised; some things are done because it is the first day of the month. These are occurrences of:

EVENTS

Each event causes something to happen – an appointment is made; an invoice is paid; a report is prepared; ie some action is taken; people carry out:

PROCESSES

Systems don't work in isolation. They have an effect on, and are affected by, other systems. A system to order books must interface in some way with systems for cataloguing and for controlling the circulation of books. A system for recording prescriptions given to patients may need to be linked to an appointments system, a recall system and to statistical systems. A pay system may interface with staff records, estimating systems, superannuation systems, and to the accounting system.

All such communication with the world outside the system being developed is by means of:

INTERFACES

Not only are things done, but if the business is to succeed, then *what* is done is not the only concern. *How well* it is done is likely to be at least as important. It is no good delivering orders randomly - they must be delivered when they are needed. And quality doesn't necessarily mean the highest quality possible; it means the quality needed for the purpose. There are times when you may want a Rolls Royce, but there are other times when a wheelbarrow will suffice. You don't need a Rolls for spreading compost. The design must achieve the required levels of:

QUALITIES

The system probably grew up over a period of time. Someone devised it and explained to the people operating it exactly what to do. This will have involved people, money, and equipment. It used:

RESOURCES

The development of a new system will also consume resources, and it is essential that these are kept under control. It is up to corporate and user management to decide how much it is willing to pay for development, how long it is prepared to wait for the system to be operational, and what are the acceptable running costs. Computers can do whatever is precisely defined for them, but the costs of ambitiously over-complex systems can be immense and take virtually forever to develop. Indefinite waits and escalating costs can drive companies to the verge of bankruptcy. This is an area that requires negotiation. Some trade-offs will almost certainly be needed between facilities, qualities, costs and time.

Summary

The six elements of a system are tabled. (*See* Table 1).

Systems analysis must establish the facts about each of these system elements.

Development costs are often closely monitored, whilst running and maintenance costs often tend to have a much lower profile. The more that is done correctly in the first place, the less it will cost over the life of the system, taking maintenance into account as well.

Table 5.1 The six elements of a system

Elements	
Data	is affected by
Events	which trigger
Processes	which have
Interfaces	with the external world. The work must be done to defined levels of
Qualities	and consume agreed levels of
Resources	commensurate with the benefits of the system.

All of the system elements are vitally important, and somehow or other all the relevant information must be collected by and understood by the analysts.

It is the purpose of SSADM to ensure the collection of this information by use of diagrams, the Requirements Catalogue, and supporting documentation. The diagrams serve two purposes:

- They provide a framework in which the information can be contained as it is found.

- The very task of constructing the diagrams prompts the questions that need to be asked.

The Requirements Catalogue permits the precise specification of:

- functional requirements, ie the processing to be carried out by the new system;

- non-functional requirements, ie the qualitative elements of the system.

Part 2

SSADM Techniques

6

The use and purpose of diagrams

INTRODUCTION

In working through a complete application of SSADM, 13 different techniques are used:

- Data Flow Modelling.

- Logical Data Modelling.

- Entity-Event Modelling.

- Requirements Definition.

- Dialogue Design.

- Business System Options.

- Technical System Options.

- Relational Data Analysis.

- Function Definition.

- Specification Prototyping.

- Physical Data Design.

- Physical Process Specification.

- Logical Database Process Design.

Of these, the principal techniques are the first three which model the system. They are diagram based and are considered in Chapters 7-9. These techniques, or something very similar, appear in other structured methods. Their effectiveness has been known for many years.

WHY USE DIAGRAMS?

The problems of communication between users and developers were mentioned earlier, as was the inadequacy of an English narrative specification of a system.

In SSADM the products of the techniques, so far as users are concerned, are diagrams rather than narrative. SSADM is a diagram-based method. It aims to help both communication and understanding by using diagramming techniques.

During the investigation the analysts construct diagrams to record their understanding of the discussions. The diagrams will be augmented with other information that the analysts find during their study. These diagrams have been shown to provide an excellent and unambiguous means of communication between users and analysts. The analysts talk through their diagrams with the users as they go about their investigations, to ensure that the information they have recorded is correct.

The diagrams, used initially for communication, fact finding, note taking and discussion, evolve as the work progresses to provide the base on which the system will be structured. They are supported by detail in other documents, but the correctness of the diagrams is the key to successful systems.

A picture, they say, is worth a thousand words. Certainly in SSADM the diagrams convey a lot of information in a simple way. The three main diagrams used during analysis in SSADM, and detailed in the following chapters, are:

- – Data Flow Diagrams (DFDs) in Chapter 7.

- – Logical Data Structures (LDS) in Chapter 8.

- – Entity Life Histories (ELHs) in Chapter 9.

DIAGRAMS AS WORKING DOCUMENTS

It is important to appreciate that the diagrams are working documents. They represent the current understanding of the system *at that point in time*. As such, they are not sacrosanct. Users must feel free to make changes to them, and such changes must be regarded as an integral part of the development process, not as the desecration of a work of art. Modifying them is 'a good thing' and is to be encouraged, with the proviso that modifications must be for correctness rather than beauty, and must fall within the agreed scope of the project. A great deal of time can be spent fruitlessly 'improving' diagrams rather than advancing knowledge. The diagrams are tools to move the analysis on towards a more complete understanding of, and ultimately to a definition of, the required system.

STANDARDS

In the diagrams and forms that follow, SSADM conventions are used in showing:

- the shape of symbols;

- upper and lower case;

- alphabetic and numeric identifiers.

Individual organisations may have their own conventions for these things. What is important is not that boxes have right-angled or rounded corners (hard boxes and soft boxes), or that an entry is made as alphabetic or numeric, or upper or lower case, but that it is always done in the same standard way, that everyone knows what the standard is, and that the standard is adhered to.

7
Data Flow Modelling — DFM

INTRODUCTION

The elements of a system were considered in Chapter 5. The analyst must elicit *all* this essential information from the user. In SSADM the starting point for the task of information gathering is by data flow modelling, part of which entails the construction of DFDs of the current system.

The objectives of the analyst are threefold:

- to obtain information from the user;

- to record the information obtained;

- to agree the record with the user.

DFDs provide the means of achieving all three of these objectives.

It is worth noting that because properly drawn DFDs are easy to understand, there is sometimes the tendency to think that they are equally easy to draw. It is certainly true that the technique is easy to apply when some experience has been gained, but there can be much agony in the early days. It is a problem similar to knowing how chess pieces can move, but not knowing how to start the game. For this reason, three additional tools are available to help in obtaining the facts and drawing them on a DFD. They are:

- The Context Diagram, essentially a very high-level DFD, which is illustrated in Figures 7.5 and 7.6.

- Document Flow Diagrams showing the movement of documentation in and out of the system, and between the various departments and people within the area to be covered by the system. They are an aid to establishing data flows.

- Resource Flow Diagrams showing the movement of physical objects rather than data. These objects will still exist after the system has been computerised. Examples are deliveries of materials (a load of bricks; a stationery order). Each diagram shows the movements of a single resource. As resources are supported by data, again they are an aid to production of data flows.

One further point to appreciate is that no matter how skilled the analyst may be, early DFDs will be incomplete and inaccurate. This is because:

— The analyst will not initially know all the questions to ask.

— The user will not recall all he knows of the system.

— The familiarity of the user with his subject may mean that he takes it for granted that the analyst understands elementary things about the system, and consequently these may not be mentioned.

— There will be misunderstandings.

The good news is that DFDs, being an excellent medium for communication, make these shortcomings apparent.

DFD SYMBOLS

DFDs are simple in concept. They consist of just six different symbols. These are illustrated in Figure 7.1.

External entities are people or organisations who send data into the system or receive data from it. Typical external entities are customer, supplier, warehouse, bank.

Processes are actions that are carried out when data is received, for example: prepare a cheque; note details of a new customer; check credit rating; issue invoice.

Data stores are groups of data, for example: customer records, paid invoices, personnel records, stock records.

The two symbols relating to resources (Resource Flow and Resource Store) are not strictly necessary. If used at all, they will only appear on the diagrams relating to the system as it currently exists.

PERMISSIBLE CONNECTIONS

Not all symbols can be connected to each other, for good reasons.

— External entities cannot be connected directly to data or resource stores. A process in the system must come between them.

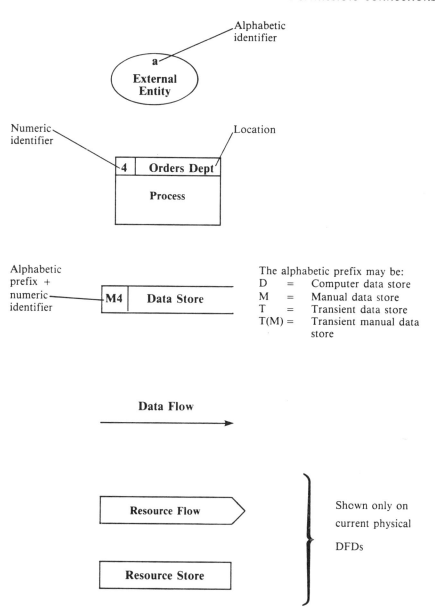

Figure 7.1 DFD symbols

– Resource stores can only be connected to processes, and only by resource flows. Obviously enough, a resource can only get into a resource store by means of a resource flow.

– External entities can be connected to each other, both by data and by resource flows. Although these are outside the system, they are included if they aid understanding.

All the permissible connections are shown in Figure 7.2.

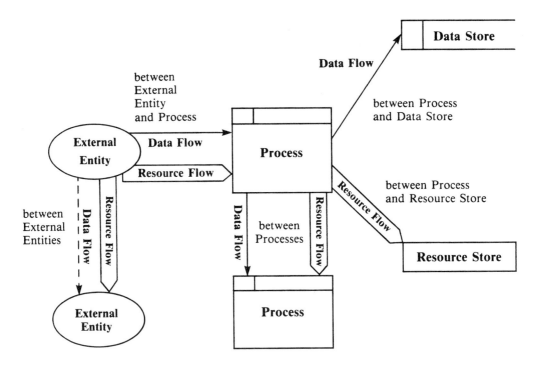

Note that stores may only be connected to processes

Figure 7.2 Permissible connections

WHAT DFDs SHOW

Their simplicity, combined with the fact that (initially) they illustrate the system as it is known to the user, ie the *current physical system,* make DFDs an ideal tool for communication.

DFDs show:

- data, both dynamic as it moves around the system in data flows, and static where data is stored;

- events, by inference from the data flows which trigger the processes;

- processes, ie what is done with the data;

- system boundaries, showing the interfaces with other systems and the outside world, ie where data comes from initially, and goes to after processing.

It can thus be seen that DFDs help to identify four of the six elements of a system (Table 5.1), which gets the analysis off to a good start.

DFD DEVELOPMENT

The early DFDs are of the current physical system (where one exists) and, as mentioned above, are inevitably incomplete.

The further development of DFDs is done in two ways:

- by transformation, progressing from the current system to the required system (*see* Transformation of DFDs);

- by decomposition, starting with a high-level view and then decomposing it into greater levels of detail (*see* Decomposition of DFDs).

Transformation of DFDs

The starting point for SSADM is the current system. This is the system as it physically exists. The aim is to replace it with a new physical system that will solve existing problems and include new requirements. DFDs help to move the analysis on from the old to the new system. This transformation is shown in Figure 7.3.

The *current physical system* DFDs record things as they are, complete with all the existing problems and inefficiencies. They show both *what* is done, and also the existing physical aspects of *where* and *how* it is done, and *who* does it.

When all the details of the current system have been investigated and recorded, the DFDs are *logicalised*. This means that the physical aspects of *who, where* and *how* are removed, leaving only *what* is done. Inefficiencies are usually found. Typically DFDs reveal:

- data that is duplicated;

- data that is input to the system and never used;

- processes currently carried out but no longer relevant;

- processes that are carried out separately, which could usefully be combined.

These inefficiencies should obviously be avoided in the new system, and are removed during *logicalisation*. The DFDs are then of the *current logical system*.

The logical system may be implemented in a variety of ways and SSADM requires alternatives to be devised. These are shown as high-level DFDs representing different business options, with variations in:

- the position of the system boundary;

- the problems to be solved;

- the new requirements that will be included;

- the quality and resource objectives that will be met.

The option selected, which may be a hybrid of those considered, becomes the *required logical system.* This gives the base from which the *required physical system* will be built.

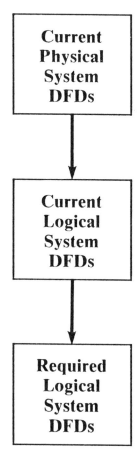

Figure 7.3 Transformation of DFDs

Decomposition of DFDs

Even superficially simple systems, when fully documented, are likely to give rise to so much information that it would be difficult to comprehend if shown in a single document. This is remedied by presenting different levels of information in different levels of diagram. This aids understanding of the system because each diagram is simple and compact. The hierarchical structure allows each user to home in on those areas of the system that are of particular interest to him, or in which he is an expert.

There are four levels of diagrams (*see* Figure 7.4):

— Context Diagram.

— Level 1 (high-level) diagram.

— Intermediate level diagrams (where three or more levels are necessary).

— Low-level diagrams, from which primary business functions (ie complete units of processing as seen by the system user) are identifiable. The objective is to decide *what* has to be done, not *how* it should be done.

These levels may (but do not necessarily) exist in all four transformations — current physical, current logical, required logical, required physical.

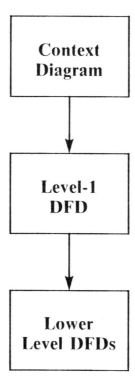

Figure 7.4 Decomposition of DFDs

DFDs ILLUSTRATED IN A LIBRARY ORDERS AND ACQUISITIONS SYSTEM

The Context Diagram

This diagram, as its name implies, puts the system in context. It contains only one box, representing the system, surrounded by external entities and the data flows to and from the system. A Context Diagram gives an excellent overview of the system.

Figure 7.5 shows the first attempt to document the items that are acquired by a public library. It was done with great rapidity and proved to be an excellent way of clarifying initial thoughts about what the system should do.

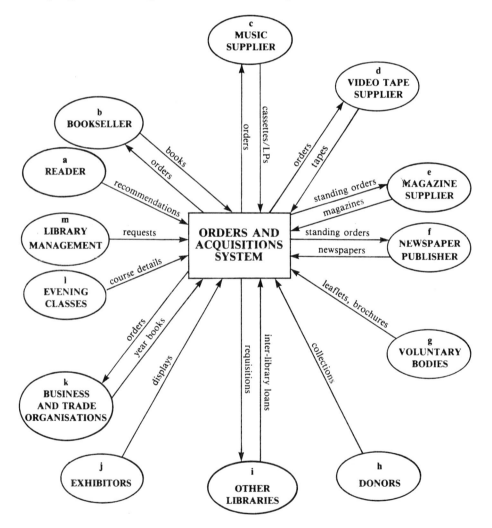

Figure 7.5 Context Diagram for a library orders and acquisitions system

It resulted in the following decisions:

- Voluntary bodies (g), exhibitors (j), and evening classes (l), being omitted as no records are maintained about them, nor will records be needed in the future. Essentially the library is merely providing publicity and services for other organisations.

- Music suppliers (c) and video tape suppliers (d) being combined as audio video suppliers. Both types of order are the same, and loans of the material are chargeable.

- Magazine suppliers (e), and newspaper publishers (f), being combined as newsagent, both being obtained by standing order and being reference material in the library.

- Reader recommendations (a) and library management requests (m), being combined as requesters, as both cause the ordering of books.

- Bookseller (b) and business and trade organisations (k), being combined as booksellers, as orders for books are placed with both.

- Other libraries (i), from which books are borrowed and returned rather than added to stock, are regarded as part of the circulation system.

These decisions resulted in the revised Context Diagram of Figure 7.6.

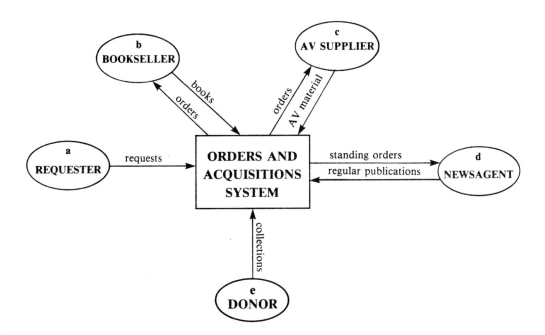

Figure 7.6 Revised Context Diagram for a library orders and acquisitions system

At this point the Context Diagram is incomplete, although it has satisfied its primary purpose of putting the system into context and setting an initial boundary for its scope. Further data flows in and out of the system will be revealed when the Level-1 DFD is constructed. The additional data flows will then be added to the Context Diagram.

Throughout a system development using SSADM, new discoveries will lead to the amplification (or correction) of earlier work.

Level-1 or High-Level Diagram

At this level the first breakdown of a system is provided. The external entities are all present as on the Context Diagram, but the system box is expanded to show the major functions and data flows within the system.

Figure 7.7 shows a Current Physical Level-1 DFD for the library orders and acquisitions system.

Drawing this diagram revealed the following data flows that had been omitted from the Context Diagram at Figure 7.6:

- notification of receipt to the requester;

- reminders to booksellers, reports from them about the order (further stock awaited; out of print and no longer available; now reprinting, etc), and payments for books received;

- reminders to audio video suppliers, reports from them, and payments to them;

- payments to newsagents;

- acknowledgements to donors or their representatives for books given to the library.

Additionally, some of the wording on data flows differed between diagrams and would need to be made the same to avoid any possibility of misunderstandings in the future. (This is a problem that would not arise with the use of most CASE tools, as they would carry the data flow notation down to the different levels of DFDs.)

Updating the Context Diagram to include these additional data flows does not move the development forward, but does make it easier for anyone joining the project to understand the work done so far. It also helps those who will eventually be involved in the maintenance of the system.

Note, this diagram may well be a totally accurate picture of what now happens. However, anyone doing quality assurance checks on the diagram would be likely to raise several queries:

- Are any reminders sent, or reports received, for orders to news-agents?

- Is there any record of periodicals on order? (In a small library, the record may be in someone's head. This may cause problems if if this person is unavailable.)

- Arc there any recently received lists for AV material or periodicals?

Resolving these queries may reveal omissions from the diagram, or prompt entries for future needs to be made in the Requirements Catalogue. If the diagram is correct, and user management do not consider future requirements to improve the service in these areas to be worth the cost, then these decisions should be documented.

Note also that the DFD shows neither priority nor sequence. Requests for books do not necessarily come in before requests for publications.

Consideration should also be provoked on how to treat the same text in different media, for example:

- some books are also available on audio tape;

- some books have been filmed and can be obtained on video tapes;

- music is available on LPs, compact disks, cassettes, sheet music, and music compilations;

although these are perhaps topics for a cataloguing system rather than an orders system.

Low-level DFDs

Each box on the high level DFD can be expanded on a separate sheet into further sub-processes, each of which may itself be subdivided, and so on. Whilst there is no limit to the number of levels to which a process may be decomposed, in practice, three levels will usually be found to suffice.

Process box 1 in Figure 7.7 has been taken down to a lower level in Figure 7.8.

The investigation of process 1 reveals that the file of request slips has been omitted from the Level-1 DFD; unless this is the same file as 'Books on Order'. The Accessions Department will need to know who has requested each item if they are to issue a notification of receipt to the requester. This implies that either details of the requester will have to be entered into the system or the request slips will have to be retained.

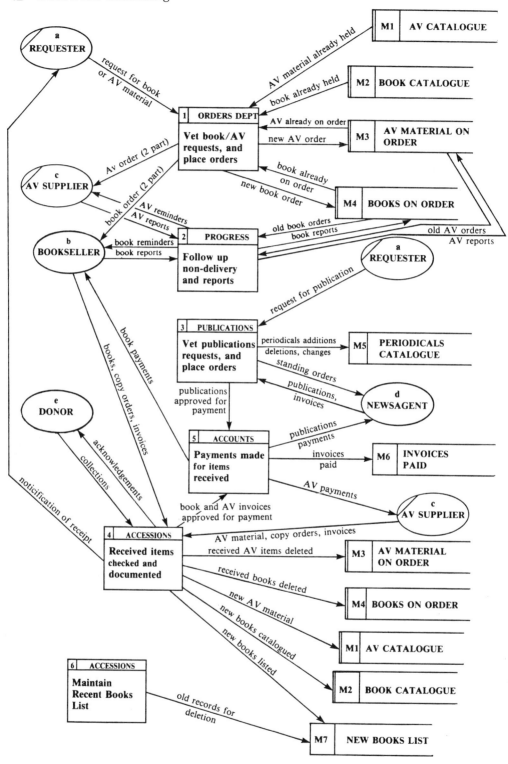

Figure 7.7 Current physical Level – 1 DFD for a library orders and acquisitions system

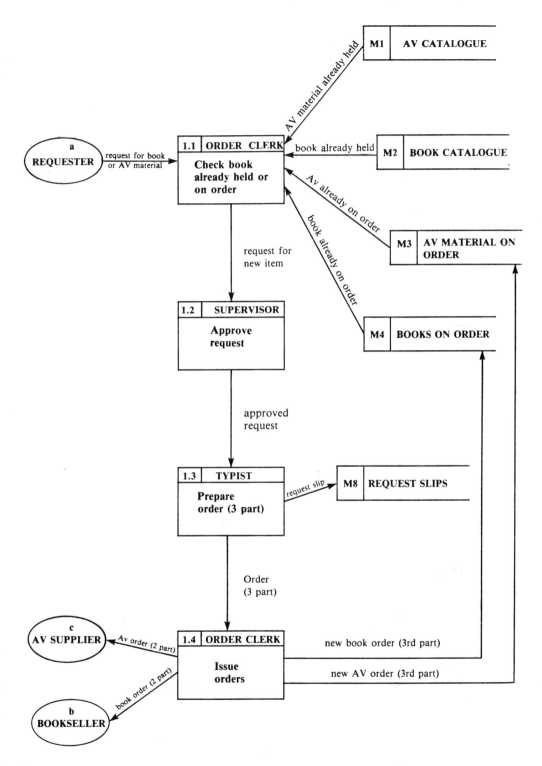

Figure 7.8 Lower level DFD for process box 1 in Figure 7.7

USES OF DFDs IN SSADM

DFDs are used throughout the application of SSADM. They are a prime source of reference, and are subject to almost constant updating as the investigation proceeds and more and more information is discovered about a system.

The DFDs of the required system should continue to be updated during subsequent maintenance. They provide an excellent overview of the system as it finally exists, and so are an ideal way for someone to learn about the system, either as a system user or as a practitioner with responsibility for maintenance.

WHAT DFDs DON'T SHOW

DFDs can only show what has been discovered. Some information will have been missed, and so the DFDs will be incomplete. The diagrams help in the identification of such instances, for example data is sometimes shown as being used, that has apparently appeared from nowhere. Other omissions may not be so readily apparent. The single viewpoint will rarely reveal all that needs to be known about a system. The complementary techniques of Logical Data Modelling and Entity-Event Modelling give two further viewpoints that will rectify most of the omissions.

Whilst DFDs show processes, they do not show their sequence or priority. It is not necessary at this stage of analysis. Also, it would complicate the diagrams and thus make them less effective for communication. Sequence and priority, which are essential for design, are established later by the Entity Life Histories (*see* Chapter 9).

The DFDs do not show system qualities and resource usage. These form a part of the Requirements Catalogue (*see* Chapter 11).

As a generalisation the DFDs only show processes that update information held within the system. Processes are excluded that merely re-sequence data or present it in reports or as screens of information. DFDs may exceptionally include this type of process if it is critical or sufficiently complex. However, retrievals shown on the early DFDs will normally be removed as part of the logicalisation process, and be included instead in the Requirements Catalogue. Eventually they will be defined as enquiry functions at Step 330 (*see* Chapter 15).

THE DATA FLOW MODEL

The DFDs are concise, precise and unambiguous. However, they do not stand alone. They are supplemented by several other documents which, together with the DFDs, go to make up the Data Flow Model:

- Elementary Process Descriptions (EPD), being detailed descriptions of the lowest level processes.

- External Entity Descriptions for each entity on the DFDs.

- I/O (Input/Output) Descriptions showing the contents of data flows which cross the system boundary.

Also, and additional to the Data Flow Model, are the:

- Data Catalogue, holding all the information about each data item in the system.

- Logical Data Store/Entity Cross-references showing the relationship between data stores on the DFDs and the corresponding entity structures on the Logical Data Model.

8

Logical Data Modelling — LDM

INTRODUCTION

Data Flow Diagrams show three aspects of data:

- what is stored;

- where it is used;

- what happens to it in the system.

In computer systems, as in manual systems, all this data will be organised into files (or a database). The task for the analyst/designer is deciding how to do this organisation. He must decide what to store and, if more than one data file will be needed, how to distribute the data between the various files. The aims are:

- to hold each item of data once only, to avoid duplication;

- to refer to the minimum number of files while doing the processing, to minimise disk accessing.

Unfortunately these are conflicting aims, and so some compromises will often be necessary in the final physical design.

The starting point for data design is the Logical Data Structure (LDS). The LDS is SSADM terminology for a diagram that, sometimes with minor variations, is also known as an Entity Relationship Model, or a Bachman Diagram. The technique for constructing it is also known as data modelling or entity modelling.

The LDS gives a top down view of the data used by the system. It is top down in that it shows logical groupings of data, without initially looking in detail at the data contents of the groups. It also shows how the groups are related to each other. An alternative view of the data (bottom up) is obtained by Relational Data

Analysis (*see* Stage 3, Step 340, *see Chapter 15*). As development proceeds, the LDS is modified and developed into the data structure from which the final physical design will be derived.

PROCESSING IN PRACTICE

If a customer places an order, then the supplier will need to hold data on both the customer (name and address) and order (what he wants). A customer may place many orders. To hold the customer's name and address with each order will duplicate the name and address within the system. This is shown in Figure 8.1.

First order	Second order	Nth order
CUSTOMER **Customer No.** **Name** **Address** **ORDER** **Order No.** **Item 1** **Item 2** . . . **Item n**	**CUSTOMER** **Customer No.** **Name** **Address** **ORDER** **Order No.** **Item 1** **Item 2** . . . **Item n**	**CUSTOMER** **Customer No.** **Name** **Address** **ORDER** **Order No.** **Item 1** **Item 2** . . . **Item n**

Figure 8.1 Multiple orders for the same customer (1)

There are three problems with this:

- it will occupy more space;

- what is meant to be the same data may not be identical;

- if the customer changed his address before delivery, there would be many different records to change.

Within the computer system the customer data would be held in one file and the order details in another. As it would then be necessary to refer from one to the other a cross-reference would be necessary, and would be achieved by noting the Customer Number on each of the order records. Figure 8.2 illustrates this.

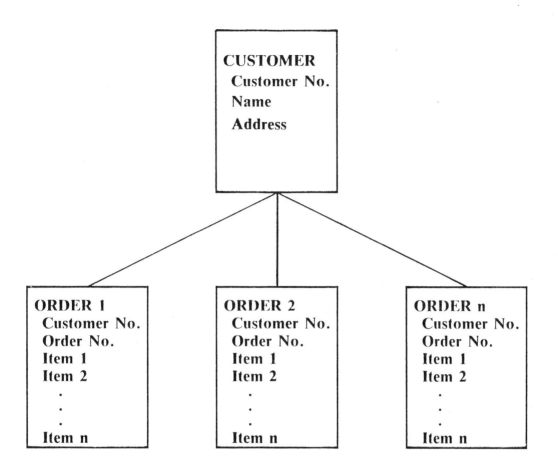

Figure 8.2 Multiple orders for the same customer (2)

ENTITIES

In computer jargon, anything about which data is stored is known as an entity. The customer is an entity, and so is an order. Clerks who have held such information in written records may be alarmed to find that they have been filing away entities all this time. Their manual records can be considered as being approximately equivalent to entities.

Each entity is represented in the system as a group of items of data (which are also known as attributes in computer jargon). Thus the entity Customer will be represented by an identifying number (Customer ID), name, address, telephone number, credit limit, etc.

In the system as it is finally developed, it is highly likely that whilst the same data may be held, it will be grouped differently in logical entities as used by the system.

Entities must be uniquely identifiable within the system. Depending upon the type of system, other typical entities are:

- supplier;

- account;

- reader;

- book;

- department.

The unique identifier for each of these is the key.

Entities are shown on the LDS as soft boxes (ie, boxes with rounded corners as shown in Figure 8.3).

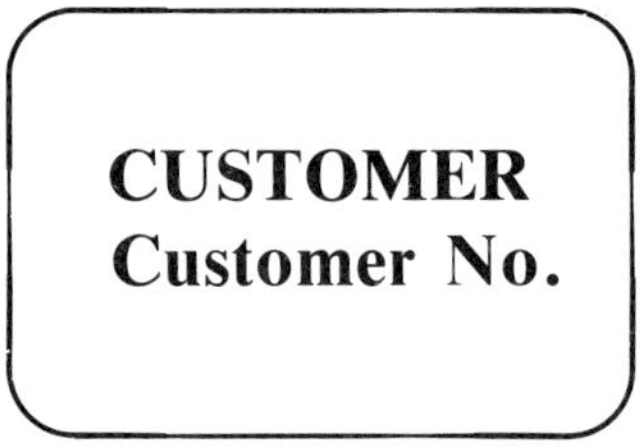

CUSTOMER
Customer No.

Figure 8.3 LDS representation of an entity

To send an order to a customer, the system will need to find the name and address from the customer file and all the orders from the orders file. The two files are thus related. The relationship is shown diagrammatically in Figure 8.4.

RELATIONSHIPS

The line joining the two entities shows that they are directly related. The degree of relationship is also shown.

There are three possible degrees of relationship between entities (*see* Figure 8.5).

The *crow's foot* indicates the *many*. The one-to-one and the many-to-many relationships are the subject of particular scrutiny during analysis, with the objective of converting them to one-to-many relationships.

The crow's foot attached to the order in Figure 8.4 indicates many, and drawing this shows that one customer may have one or more orders.

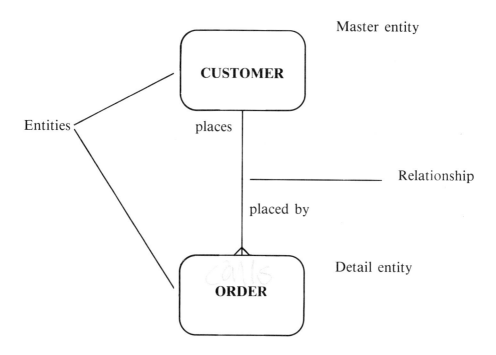

Figure 8.4 The relationship between customer and order

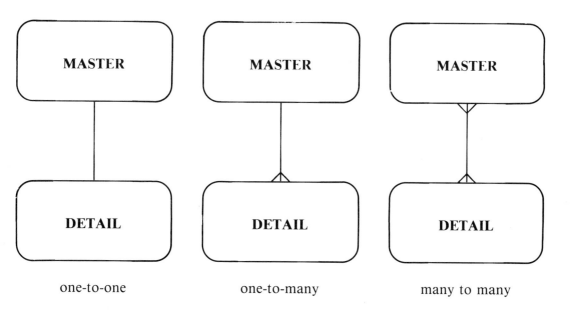

Figure 8.5 Degrees of relationship between entities

The diagram tells the designer that:

— he will need to have two files;

— that to make up an order the system will need to look at both files;

— there must be a cross-reference between them.

Relationship link phrases

Each relationship is described by a phrase that indicates the nature of the relationship between the two entities. In Figure 8.4, the phrases show that the customer places orders, and that orders are placed by the customer. These phrases are then formalised into relationship statements that specify the relationship in terms that are both precise and unambiguous, for example, *each order must be placed by one and only one customer.*

THE LDS DEPENDS ON REQUIREMENTS

The relationship between entities will vary depending on the system requirements. Extending Figure 8.4 to include the issue of invoices could result in any of the relationships in Figure 8.6.

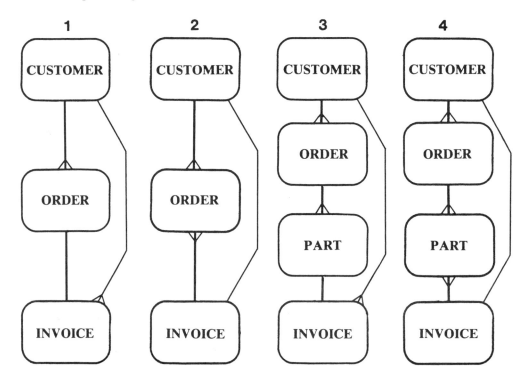

Figure 8.6 Relationships depend on requirements

The different system requirements are:

1   Each order to be completely filled and a separate invoice to be issued for each separate order processed that day.

2   Each order to be completely filled and one invoice to be issued for all orders processed that day.

3   Orders may be sent out part filled, with a separate invoice for each part.

4   Orders may be part filled, but with one invoice for all orders processed that day.

In each instance, no historical records of orders or invoices are to be kept.

AN LDS FOR A LIBRARY ORDERS AND AQUISITIONS SYSTEM

Figure 7.7 showed the current physical system Level-1 DFD for a library orders and acquisitions system. The library has decided that every item ordered should be prepared on an individual form. Thus if two copies of the same book are ordered, two separate order forms will be created, even if both are going to the same bookseller. This:

—   permits the supplier to send one copy of an order back with each item supplied, which assists in control;

—   removes the need to cater for partial orders being supplied;

—   permits the orders for two identical items to be placed with different suppliers, so that comparisons can be made between the service provided by each.

When the analyst constructs the LDS it could look something like Figure 8.7.

RELATIONSHIP WITH THE DFDs

As both the DFD and the LDS show data, there is clearly a connection between the two. The data stores on the DFD are approximately equivalent to the entities on the LDS.

Inevitably in drawing the two separately, a comparison between the two is likely to reveal omissions from both. The DFD and LDS must contain the same information in total and the data structure on the LDS must permit the processing indicated on the DFD. Thus the two diagrams are complementary.

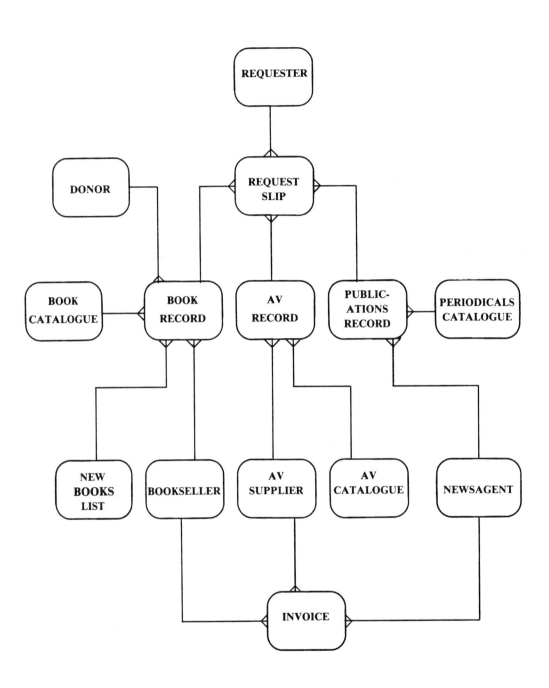

Figure 8.7 LDS for a library orders and acquisitions system

A comparison of the LDS with the DFDs shows that several LDS entities are not shown as data stores. The possibilities are:

- they have been missed by the analyst who drew up the DFD; or

- they are not entities, and should not be present on the LDS.

Five of the omissions are:

- AV supplier;

- Bookseller;

- Donor;

- Newsagent;

- Requester.

These appear on the DFD as external entities. External entities can be expected to be represented within a system as data stores, and an experienced analyst would have been unlikely to have missed them all. However, not all analysts are experienced, and this comparison shows that what is missed by one technique can be picked up by another.

The other entity shown on the LDS but not on the DFDs is Publications Record. A copy order is held in the library for each publication ordered, and was missed when the DFD was drawn up. Again, a further data store must be added to the DFD.

An important lesson for managers is that there is no need to strive for absolute perfection in the end product of one technique before going on to the next. continuing with the analysis techniques will pick up omissions, even from diagrams that were thought to be complete and correct when they were drawn up.

COMPLEX RELATIONSHIPS

The examples given in this chapter are necessarily simple ones to illustrate the technique. The LDS for a real system would be likely to contain many entities, and more information about the relationships between them, which may be:

- multiple (more than one relationship between the same two entities);

- optional (the relationship may exist, as compared with those for which a relationship must exist);

- exclusive (relationships may be with more than one other entity, but only with one at any one time);

- recursive (the relationship is with itself), for example, a middle manager will manage others, but will also himself be managed.

The diagram may also be annotated with volumetric information (How many of each? How often? When? etc).

THE LOGICAL DATA MODEL

The LDS shows the names of the entities, but not the detail they contain. The LDS is therefore supplemented by other documents to make up the Logical Data Model:

- Entity Descriptions (including details of the data held for each entity, and relationships with other entities).

- Relationship Descriptions (details of every relationship on the LDS, with two forms for each, ie, one for each entity).

Also, and additional to the Logical Data Model, are the:

- Data Catalogue (which was also mentioned as supplementing the Data Flow Model). This contains the following:

  - Attribute/Data Item Descriptions (information about each element of data);

  - Grouped Domain Descriptions (for attributes of identical format or with identical validation rules, for example, dates. Several different dates may be held within a record, for example, date of birth, date employment started, dates of promotions).

- Logical Data Store/Entity Cross-reference (showing the correspondence between data stores on the DFDs and entities on the LDS).

- Enquiry Access Paths (showing the routes through the LDS to satisfy each of the enquiries).

9
Entity-Event Modelling — EEM

INTRODUCTION

The Data Flow Diagrams show processes, but give no indication of sequence or priority, and data, but not in any sort of structured way.

The LDS puts a structure on the data and cross checks against the DFDs, but does not show how data changes over a period of time.

Entity Life Histories (ELHs), created during EEM, give a visual picture of each entity, and put a time structure on every event that may affect an entity throughout its existence in the system. Thus they put a sequence on the processes on the DFDs.

An ELH therefore relates to the LDS, there being one ELH for each entity on the LDS. Also, events identified during EEM correspond to the data flows on the DFDs (except for system generated events, for example, events triggered by time, or by information generated within the system). Thus all three of the major diagramming techniques complement each other. Between them they ensure that there is very little of any significance that escapes the very tight analysis net which SSADM casts around the system.

AN ENTITY LIFE

The idea of entity life histories is essentially a simple one. Every entity in the system must initially be created (its birth). Then, while it is of use within the system, it will be affected by a number of events (its life). Ultimately it will leave the system (its death). This is illustrated in Figure 9.1, which shows the life cycle of an entity, documented diagrammatically as an ELH.

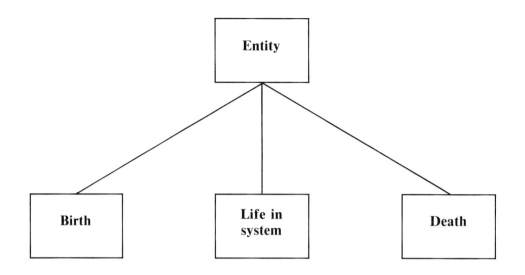

Figure 9.1 An entity life

ELH CONSTRUCTS

In the simplest ELH, events happen in a strict sequence. A person can open a
bank account, then put money in, then make withdrawals, and eventually close
the account. A sequence is illustrated in Figure 9.2.

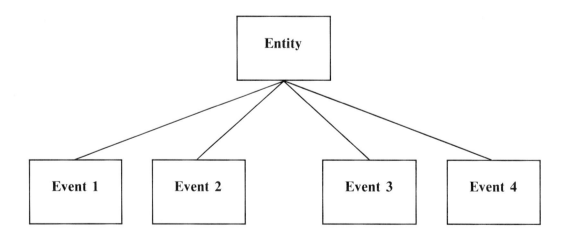

Figure 9.2 A sequence of events
Event 1, followed by Event 2, followed by Event 3, followed by Event 4.

Sometimes there will be a choice of events. This is known as a selection. The account holder may make either a deposit or a withdrawal. Selection is shown in Figure 9.3, and is indicated by an 'o' in the top right hand corner of the box.

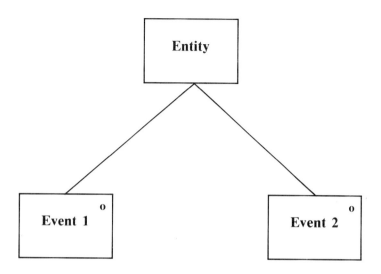

Figure 9.3 A selection: either Event 1 or Event 2

Some transactions can occur more than once — an iteration. A person may make a whole series of deposits and withdrawals. Iteration is shown in Figure 9.4 by the * in the top right hand corner of the box.

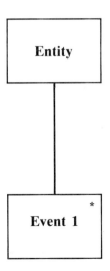

Figure 9.4 An iteration: Event 1 can occur many times

All three of these constructs are shown in Figure 9.5, which shows a much simplified ELH for a bank account.

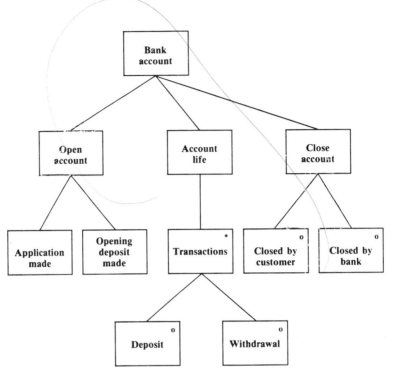

Figure 9.5 A simplified ELH for a bank account

AN ELH WITHIN A LIBRARY ORDERS AND ACQUISITIONS SYSTEM

Figure 9.6 shows an ELH for the library system entity Request Slip.

Besides the representations for sequence, selection and iteration, two further notations are shown.

Effect Qualifiers

The two events *Order required* and *No order required* are each shown twice on the diagram. In order to differentiate between them, an effect qualifier is shown in brackets. This is necessary because the action taken will be different where no order is required. In the first instance, the requester must be notified that the book will not be ordered. In the second, he can be told that a copy is already held or on order, and that he will be notified when it is available for loan.

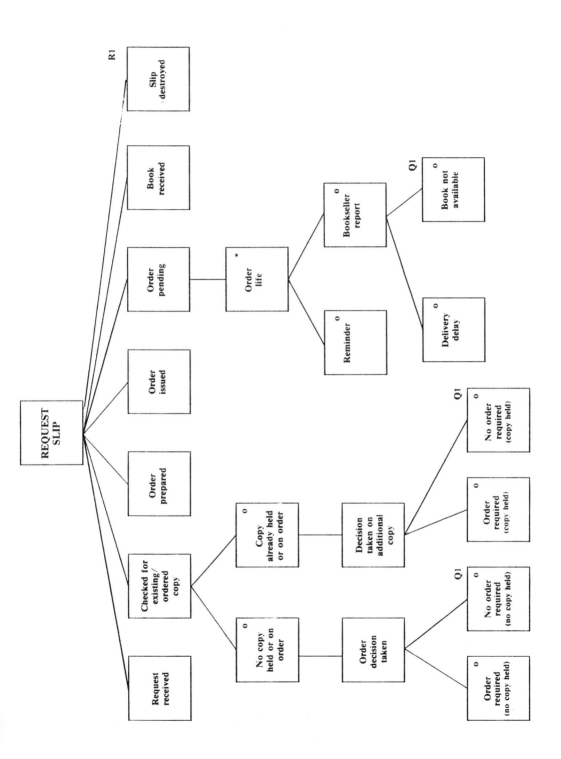

Figure 9.6 ELH for library orders and acquisitions system Request Slip

Quits and Resumes

Sometimes an event occurs that interrupts the normal sequence of events and causes a jump in the sequence, either to somewhere later in the sequence, or shown in separate boxes off the main diagram. This is shown in three places on Figure 9.6, where the normal life is terminated early. These are indicated by the notation Q1 on each. Further action for each of them is resumed at R1.

Comparison with the DFDs

Once again a comparison with the DFDs reveals that the data flows indicated by R1, R2 and R3 are missing and should be inserted.

ELHs IN PRACTICE

Whilst simple in concept, ELHs are time-consuming to produce. The work is detailed and painstaking, and can be expected to reveal a significant number of omissions from the DFDs. These omissions are the sort of thing that often, in a 'traditional' approach to systems analysis, only become visible during programming, user acceptance testing, or even after implementation. Changes during these later stages of system development can be very expensive indeed – far in excess of the time spent on constructing the ELHs.

Inevitably there can be complications:

– The same event may affect different occurrences of an entity in different ways, depending on the circumstances. For example, payment of a standing order will result in a debit from one account and a credit to another account.

– Events may be presented to the system in an unacceptable sequence. State Indicators are entered on the diagram to show the current state of an entity (ie where it is in its life cycle). These indicators can then be checked during processing to ensure that incoming transactions are being received in the correct sequence.

OPERATIONS

The diagrams are further augmented by the allocation of operations to the lowest level boxes. These cater for the birth effect, the amendment of records, and for the establishment and changing of relationships. A set of logical operations is set out in the *SSADM Manual*.

EFFECT CORRESPONDENCE DIAGRAMS

Effect Correspondence Diagrams (ECDs) are the converse of ELHs.

An ELH shows how one entity is affected by many events. It establishes the correct sequence for the processing, and aims to ensure that no processing is missed.

An ECD shows how one event can affect many entities. It is effectively a subset of the LDS, and with the same aims — to establish the access paths needed to carry out the processing of each event. It provides the information needed for the development of Update Process Models that go forward into physical design.

10
The three viewpoints

INTRODUCTION

The last three chapters considered the three main diagrammatic techniques used in SSADM. These techniques are complementary. Each has given its own view of the system. Each, alone, has helped to increase knowledge of the system, but each, individually, is an incomplete representation of the system.

The examples of diagrams created for a library orders and acquisitions system showed that each of the later diagrams revealed omissions from DFDs. It can be argued that this would not be the case if the DFDs had been done 'properly' in the first place. Unfortunately, humans are fallible, and things do get missed.

DRAWING A COMPARISON

Comparing the diagrams with each other helps to find discrepancies, and fill in blanks. There is absolutely no need to agonise indefinitely on fruitless attempts at getting each diagram to a state of absolute perfection that would usually be beyond attainment. You can confidently expect that what is missed by one approach will be picked up by one of the others.

You could, for example, after taking your first studied consideration of DFDs, spend many more man weeks on them for a minimal gain in information, but reaching the stage where it seemed that perfection had been achieved. Then construction of ELHs could reveal perhaps another 25 percent of information that had been missing from the DFDs.

Whilst it might seem that the more detailed approach to analysis as required by SSADM will be unnecessarily time-consuming, there are two factors that prevent it from being so:

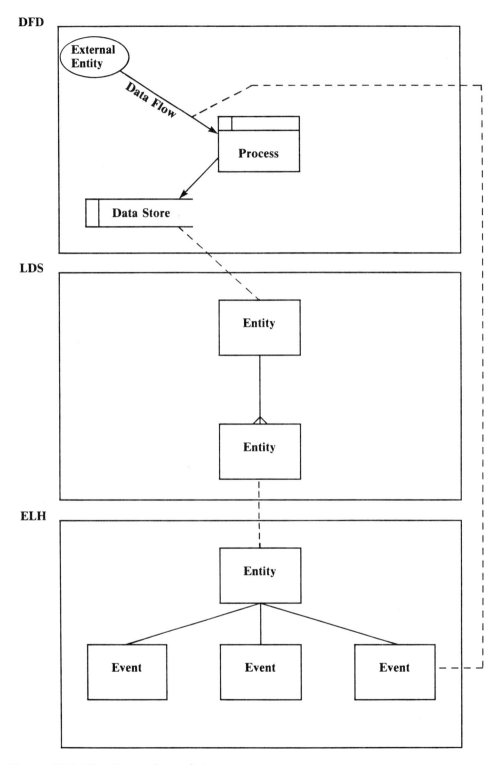

Figure 10.1 The three viewpoints

— the time spent on the individual tasks will not be excessive if full advantage is taken of their complementary nature mentioned above, given sensible management to keep things moving along;

— the time spent is, in fact, a displacement of effort from the later stages where it is wasteful, to the earliest stage where it is more cost-effective.

Information which can be cross-checked between diagrams is:

— entities on the LDS must be represented somewhere in the data stores on the DFDs;

— events on the ELH will match data flows which trigger processes on the DFDs;

— entities on the ELHs will correspond to entities on the LDS.

The approach is very thorough and not much should be missed. The relationships between these techniques are illustrated in Figure 10.1.

11

The Requirements Catalogue

INTRODUCTION

The Requirements Catalogue is the fourth major piece of the jigsaw that completes the picture needed by the system designers. The other three pieces are all diagrammatic ones – DFDs, the LDS and ELHs. The Requirements Catalogue is needed to allow for the entry of things considered wrong with the current system, and all the things it would be desirable to have in the new system.

Each Catalogue entry is made on a separate sheet, thus permitting groupings such as priorities and related requirements.

It may not be too difficult to set out the functional requirements, ie *what* the system is to do. It is often rather more difficult to deal with the non-functional requirements, ie *how well* the system is to perform, and *what* resource usage is permissible. Yet it is often the *how well* rather than the *what* that decides whether the system is acceptable to its users.

There is always some limit to resources. Real world considerations of development time and cost will determine how closely the final system can match the entries in the Requirements Catalogue. This should not inhibit entries from being made in the Catalogue based on assumptions of what will be possible and practical. The assumptions may be wrong. The bases for the assumptions may change whilst development is in progress.

Anything included from the start is likely to cost very much less to implement than if requested after the system has been installed. An entry in the Requirements Catalogue, even if not implemented initially, will alert the developers to a possible future enhancement. Hooks for it can be built into the initial design, so that later implementation of the feature can be done at minimum cost.

ALLOCATING PRIORITIES

Accepting that not every item in the Requirements Catalogue will be implemented initially, it will be necessary to decide the importance of each. When allocating priorities, it is easy to be too ambitious. At least to begin with, a very modest categorisation of priorities will usually be adequate, for example:

- mandatory;

- desirable; or

- high;

- medium;

- low.

These priorities can then be set against the resource levels needed to implement the items, either initially or in later enhancements to the system. Items for initial implementation are likely to be those with either high priority or low cost, with a sprinkling of medium priority/medium cost items.

PRECISION IN REQUIREMENTS

Initially, entries in the Requirements Catalogue can be quite woolly, eg 'More information is needed on the Despatch Note', 'The trial balance must be available sooner', etc. Sometimes systems are built on such requirements. They are seldom satisfactory. Imprecise requirements are fine as a starting point - a note to ensure that nothing is forgotten. They must be made precise when the Requirements Catalogue is considered in more detail at Step 120 (Chapter 13) and when defining various Business System Options at Step 210 (Chapter 14).

An entry such as 'The response should be faster', must be amplified to something like:

'Within the peak times of

09.15 to 09.45

12.00 to 14.00

17.00 to 18.00

the response time must be less than 4 seconds. Outside those times the response must be less than 9 seconds.'

This gives the designer a target to aim at. He will need to ensure that the design can meet these requirements. It will provide a yardstick against which the performance of the delivered system can be measured for acceptability.

SPECIFYING REQUIREMENTS IN A MEASURABLE WAY

For each of the critical objectives, consider:

- a definition of the objectives;

- how they will be specified;

- the current situation, for purposes of comparison.

- a *precise* specification of the requirements. They should be stated in a way that is unambiguous, and measurable or provable where possible, avoiding generalities such as better, faster, more detail, etc. The limits of tolerance should be stated wherever possible, ie:

  - least acceptable: anything below this would provide grounds for rejection of the system;

  - the target level of performance;

  - best usable;

  - references to other documentation that supports the facts and objectives.

PRINCIPAL USES OF THE REQUIREMENTS CATALOGUE WITHIN SSADM

The Requirements Catalogue features throughout the application of SSADM. Thoughts can occur at any time, and the Catalogue is constantly available for enhancement. However, the principal times when it is at the centre of activities are described in Part 3, Chapters 12 – 18. They are:

- Step 010 when it is first set up.

- Step 020 when attempts are made to define problems and requirements.

- Step 030 for decisions on the minimum requirements of any new system.

- Step 110 when it is first set up if there has been no Feasibility Study.

- Step 120 where it is expanded as a result of more detailed analysis work, and priorities are assigned.

- Step 210 in which the Catalogue is again considered in the light of additions that have been made to it. Items and their priorities are checked, and possible solutions are considered and recorded. In particular, the base constraints are identified. These are the constraints that must apply to all the Business System Options.

- Step 310 to identify items that have been excluded from the Selected Business System Option and to note the reasons.

- Step 350 when some changes may be necessary following experience of the prototyping exercise.

- Step 370 during which each entry is checked to ensure that it has been fully defined.

- Step 410 when it is considered during preparation of the Technical System Options.

- Steps 640 and 660 where steps are taken to ensure that the design will meet the objectives specified in the Catalogue.

Part 3

SSADM Activities

12
Stage 0 – Feasibility

INTRODUCTION

Stage 0 consists of four steps. Its aim is to establish whether the proposed system development should go ahead (at least as far as the next stage). To do this it must decide:

- who will be involved;

- what options there are;

- what costs and timescales are involved;

- whether the system will be an effective one for the organisation.

It does this by taking a high-level view of the work that is done in much more detail in Stages 1–4 of the full method.

The Feasibility Study is not mandatory in SSADM, but its omission should carry a system health warning. Much of the work done in the Feasibility Study will save a corresponding amount of work in a subsequent full study. More importantly, it disposes, relatively cheaply, of projects that should go no further. Projects tend to gather momentum once they have got under way. It takes a brave decision to stop a full study that should never have started in the first place. Stage 0 is illustrated in Figure 12.1.

STEP 010   PREPARE FOR THE FEASIBILITY STUDY

This is the introductory overview step. It takes a preliminary view of the proposed system, and lays down the plans for the rest of the study.

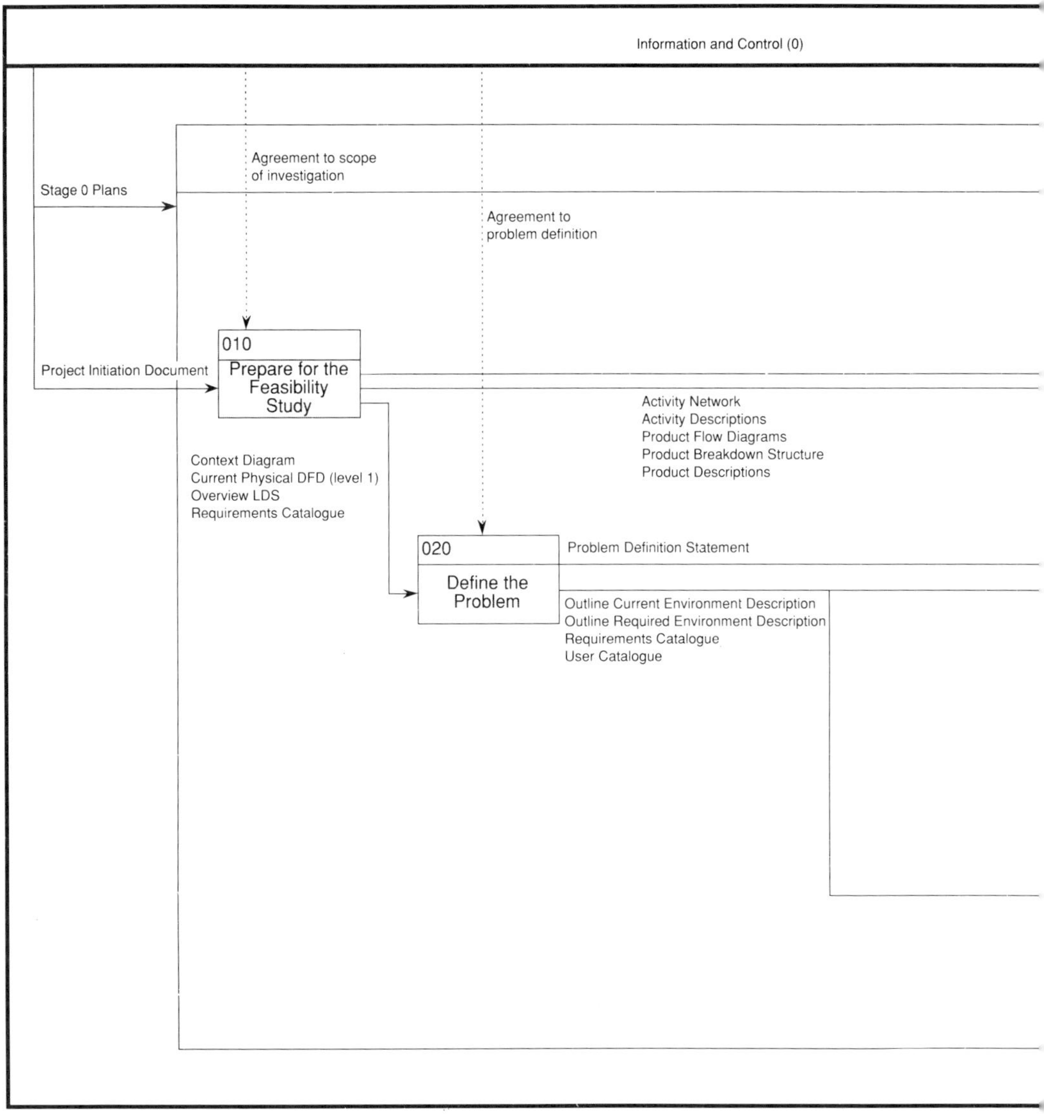

Information and Control (0)

Agreement to scope
of investigation

Stage 0 Plans

Agreement to
problem definition

Project Initiation Document

010
Prepare for the
Feasibility
Study

Activity Network
Activity Descriptions
Product Flow Diagrams
Product Breakdown Structure
Product Descriptions

Context Diagram
Current Physical DFD (level 1)
Overview LDS
Requirements Catalogue

020
Define the
Problem

Problem Definition Statement

Outline Current Environment Description
Outline Required Environment Description
Requirements Catalogue
User Catalogue

Figure 12.1 Stage 0

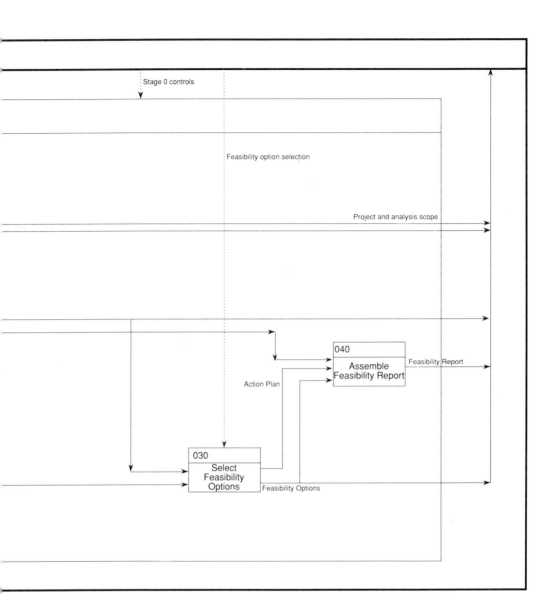

Crown Copyright July 1990 – SSADM Version 4

The Project Initiation Document is reviewed to assess the scope of the project. This includes the creation of:

- Context Diagram.

- Current Physical DFD (level 1).

- Overview LDS.

- Requirements Catalogue.

The project is planned and scheduled, and the proposals are agreed with the project board.

STEP 020   DEFINE THE PROBLEM

Given the approval for the study to proceed, more information is now gathered to add to the understanding of the business, its current problems and future requirements. This entails:

- production of a Level 1 DFD for the required environment, proceeding to lower levels for processes where the situation warrants it;

- updating of the other documents;

- identifying and entering details of intended users in a User Catalogue.

The requirements are then set out in a Problem Definition Statement, which again requires the agreement of the project board before proceeding with the study.

STEP 030   SELECT FEASIBILITY OPTIONS

There are likely to be many ways in which a system could be implemented:

- the boundary between what the computer will do and what people (or other systems) will do can be drawn in different places;

- the current problems to be solved and the new requirements to be included can be varied;

- the system if computerised, can be implemented in different ways – centralised or distributed, conventional files or database, PCs or mainframes, customised or package, etc.

In Step 030 several options are generated, first from the business viewpoint, then their technical implementation. Options are discussed with users to produce a short list, ideally of three options. Plans for the development of each of these are prepared and submitted to the project board for consideration. This may well produce a further composite option.

STEP 040   ASSEMBLE FEASIBILITY FEPORT

The Feasibility Study ends with the preparation of the Feasibility Report. Some revision is likely to be necessary as a result of the decisions made in Step 030. A final check is then made of all the current documentation. The documents are checked for conformance with SSADM and with organisational standards, and are cross-checked for consistency. When the work has passed these quality checks it is assembled into the Feasibility Report. A management decision to go ahead must then be taken before work can continue on the detailed study that starts in Stage 1.

13

Stage 1 – Investigation of Current Environment

INTRODUCTION

Stage 1 is the first stage in a full investigation. Reference is made in the following sections to the creation of documents. However, when a Feasibility Study has been undertaken, some of this documentation will already exist.

Usually the system under consideration will already exist, but not be working satisfactorily. This provides the starting point for the study.

Much of the first step is concerned with non-SSADM activities, ie the planning, estimating and scheduling of the work. The stage proceeds in Steps 120 to 140 with the SSADM techniques being applied in a top-down way, starting with high level views of the system, and proceeding down to detail. The physical elements are then removed from the Data Flow Diagrams to give a logical view of the current system. (*See* Figure 13.1).

STEP 110   ESTABLISH ANALYSIS FRAMEWORK

The work in this step is very similar to that carried out at Step 010, and the products are the same, ie:

- Context Diagram.

- Current physical DFD (Level 1).

- Overview LDS.

- Requirements Catalogue.

The starting point is the Project Initiation Document and plans, together with the documentation created during any study that may have been carried out.

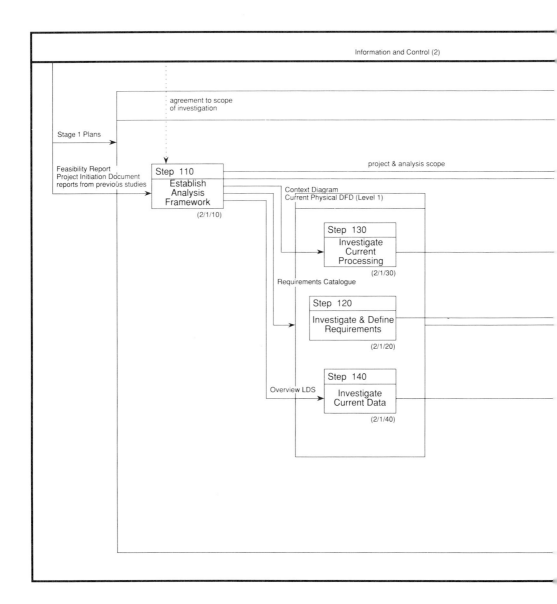

Figure 13.1 Stage 1

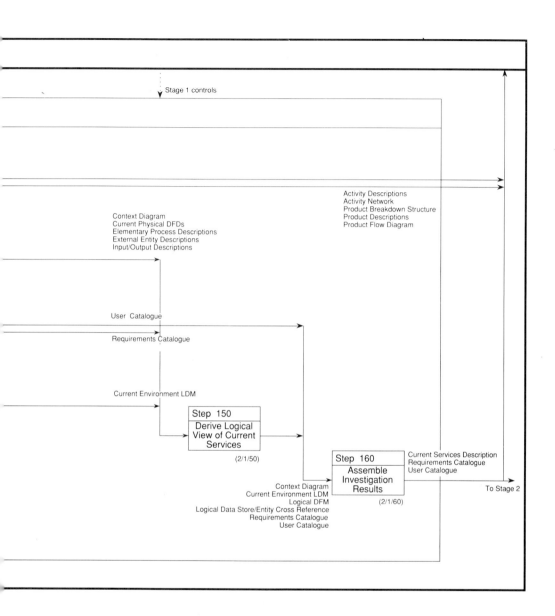

Stage 1 controls

Activity Descriptions
Activity Network
Product Breakdown Structure
Product Descriptions
Product Flow Diagram

Context Diagram
Current Physical DFDs
Elementary Process Descriptions
External Entity Descriptions
Input/Output Descriptions

User Catalogue

Requirements Catalogue

Current Environment LDM

Step 150
Derive Logical
View of Current
Services

(2/1/50)

Step 160
Assemble
Investigation
Results

(2/1/60)

Current Services Description
Requirements Catalogue
User Catalogue

Context Diagram
Current Environment LDM
Logical DFM
Logical Data Store/Entity Cross Reference
Requirements Catalogue
User Catalogue

To Stage 2

If an SSADM Feasibility Study has been done, then the Feasibility Report will be reviewed at this point. Requirements may have changed, some updating of the technical documents may be necessary, and estimates of the costs and benefits must be reconsidered. The outputs from this step, including the detailed plans for the scope of the work, are considered by the project board.

STEP 120   INVESTIGATE AND DEFINE REQUIREMENTS

Step 120 is carried out concurrently with Steps 130 and 140. During these three steps the overview of the system, taken in Step 110, is amplified as the investigation proceeds and more detail is obtained.

Step 120 is concerned with requirements and the consequent entries in the Requirements Catalogue. Initial information will come directly from the users: details of problems they have currently, and what additional facilities they want from the new system. This will be augmented by further problems and requirements that come to light as the processing is considered in more detail in Step 130 and the data structure is refined in Step 140.

The involvement of the users is essential in this step, and so one of the tasks to be undertaken is to identify all the users of the system. Details are entered in the User Catalogue, identifying them by job title and the activities that each of them carries out.

There are three main points to be made about entries in the Requirements Catalogue:

- The entries must be prioritised (this can be on any scale, although the more sophisticated the priorities, the more effort it will take for perhaps little payoff. Mandatory, desirable and optional may suffice, at least initially).

- For the most critical entries, possible solutions should be noted.

- Entries relating to qualities and resources should be both quantifiable and measurable (how well and how much). Note that more work may be entailed in providing a means of making the measurement.

STEP 130   INVESTIGATE CURRENT PROCESSING

Step 130 is carried out concurrently with Steps 120 and 140. This is because investigation of the processing will reveal new requirements, and the data model developed at Step 140 must support the processing that is being investigated at Step 130.

At this time the investigation is of the system as it currently exists. The starting point for the documentation is the Current Physical Data Flow Diagram

(Level 1), created in Step 110. Whilst DFDs can be drawn directly, in the early stages of a system study they are inevitably incomplete, and this is not self-evident from an inspection of the diagrams. As an aid to extracting the maximum amount of information as early as possible in the study, Document Flow Diagrams are developed from, and are used to enhance, the Level 1 DFD.

The investigation continues with the preparation of lower level DFDs – Level 2, and lower levels where necessary. Elementary Process Descriptions are created for the processes on the lowest level DFDs. Input/Output Descriptions are produced for flows across the system boundary, and External Entity Descriptions are produced for the entities outside the boundary.

STEP 140   INVESTIGATE CURRENT DATA

Step 140 is carried out concurrently with Steps 120 and 130. Completion of all three of these steps marks the end of the investigation into the current physical system.

The current Logical Data Structure to be documented is that needed to support the processing as it is shown in the Current Physical Data Flow Diagrams. It is independent of the way in which the data is currently organised. Data needed for new requirements is not included.

A start is made on Entity Descriptions, defining their most significant attributes, but making no attempt to be comprehensive.

This work is likely to give rise to further entries in the Requirements Catalogue.

STEP 150   DERIVE LOGICAL VIEW OF CURRENT SERVICES

The diagrams produced up to this point have been derived from the investigation of the current physical system, with all its inadequacies. Little is achieved by computerising a mess, other than to obtain a computerised mess. The first step towards improving the situation is achieved by removing the physical constraints from the work done thus far.

Logicalisation is done on the lowest level DFDs, with changes being carried back up into the higher level diagrams. The supporting documents (Elementary Process Descriptions, Input/Output Descriptions, External Entity Descriptions and the Requirements Catalogue) are also amended as necessary to reflect the logical view of the system.

STEP 160   ASSEMBLE INVESTIGATION RESULTS

The final step in Stage 1 is a comprehensive review of all the documentation that has been produced. Up to this point, checking has been principally of individual documents. One of the strengths of SSADM is the way in which the different documents complement each other, and so Step 160 carries out comprehensive cross checks between them. The involvement of the users is essential for the eventual development of a successful system.

The review procedure is not defined within SSADM. Organisations that do not have an existing procedure are recommended to adopt one of the formal approaches to this task. (Inspections are outlined in Chapter 20.) Errors and misunderstandings that can be corrected at this point will be vastly cheaper to implement than if found at a later stage in development.

Corrections required as a result of the review are completed. The project can then advance to Stage 2.

14

Stage 2 – Business System Options

INTRODUCTION

The aim of systems analysis and design is to specify a system that will satisfy the users' requirements. When a system solution appears on the horizon, there can be a tendency not to look any further. However it would be rare indeed to find that there was only one possible solution that would be of use to the users.

Stage 2 recognises this and sets out specifically to generate several different solutions, all satisfying any mandatory constraints but with different variations on system boundaries, facilities included, requirements satisfied and problems solved. (*See* Figure 14.1).

STEP 210   DEFINE BUSINESS SYSTEM OPTIONS

The various requirements of the new system will have different priorities, ranging from those that are essential to those that it would be nice to have some day. The essential requirements are identified. All solutions must satisfy these mandatory features. Within these constraints there are likely to be many possibilities with different costs and benefits. Each of perhaps six possibilities is put forward in outline as a Business System Option. These are reduced to two or three after discussion with users.

Each of the short listed options is developed in more detail, including cost/benefit analyses and organisational implications.

STEP 220   SELECT BUSINESS SYSTEM OPTION

The Requirements Analysis Module culminates in the presentation of the short listed Business System Options to the project board, and to a wider audience where appropriate.

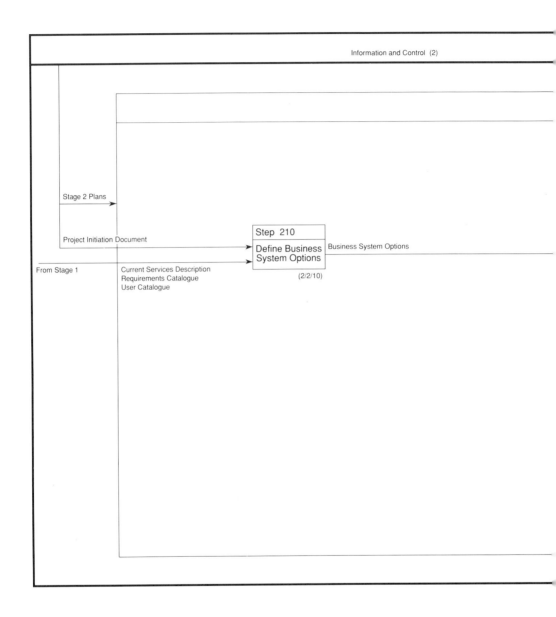

Figure 14.1 Stage 2

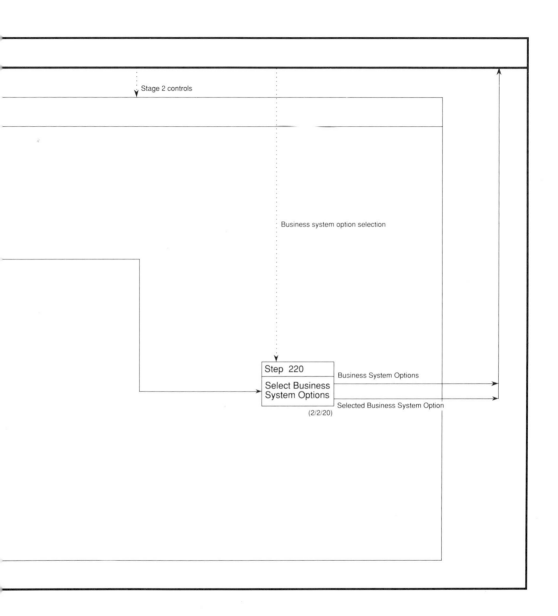

Stage 2 controls

Business system option selection

Step 220

Select Business
System Options

(2/2/20)

Business System Options

Selected Business System Option

The analysts can only present the options and their implications. The actual selection is a business decision to be taken by the sponsors of the project. The selected option could be one of those presented, but is quite likely to be a hybrid. It could contain elements from more than one of the options presented, and maybe some new ideas that arise during the presentation process.

After the choice has been made, a description is developed for the selected option, and this goes forward to the Requirements Specification Module.

15

Stage 3 – Definition of Requirements

INTRODUCTION

Stage 3 is the only stage in the Requirements Specification Module. During this stage, the selected BSO is transformed into the Requirements Specification. The Data Flow Diagrams provide the source of information for functions. The data structure is improved by relational data analysis. Further detail about events, effects, and hence processing, are obtained from the development of Entity Life Histories.

STEP 310   DEFINE REQUIRED SYSTEM PROCESSING

This step involves the Data Flow Diagrams and related documents. The work is done concurrently with Step 320.

The DFDs are updated in the light of the selected Business System Option. This in turn will cause changes to the Requirements Catalogue, Elementary Process Descriptions, Input/Output (I/O) Descriptions, and External Entity Descriptions.

Data store contents are compared with the Logical Data Model.

User roles are defined in the required system.

STEP 320   DEVELOP REQUIRED DATA MODEL

Step 320 is carried out concurrently with step 310. The Logical Data Model and Requirements Catalogue are updated and the structure is checked to ensure that it supports the Elementary Process Descriptions.

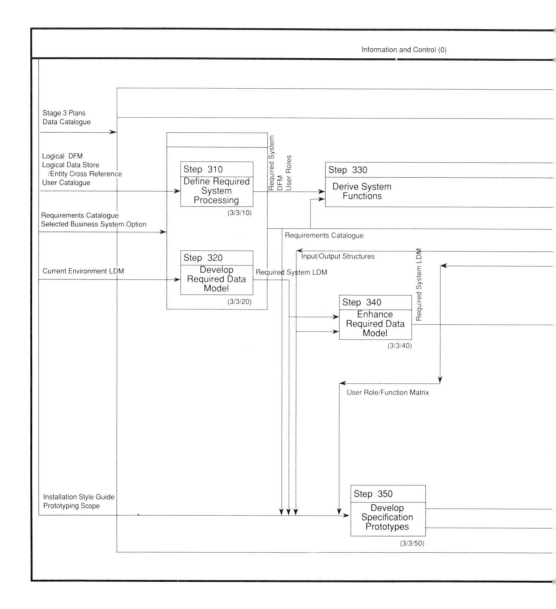

Figure 15.1 Stage 3

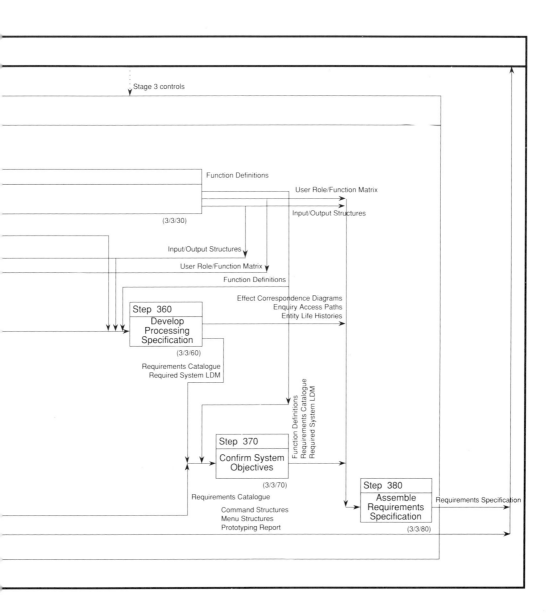

STEP 330   DERIVE SYSTEM FUNCTIONS

In this step a significant transformation takes place. The Required System Data Flow Diagrams provide the source of information for the creation of update Function Definitions (more are likely to be found later when Entity Life Histories are created at Step 360). Enquiry Function Definitions are derived mainly from the Requirements Catalogue. (Some of the more critical or complex enquiries may be shown on the DFDs.)

With the functions established, the user interface is now defined as Input/Output Structures. For updates, these come from the Input/Output Descriptions in the Data Flow Model. The enquiry interfaces are established from discussions with users. System dialogues are identified from completion of the User Role/Function Matrix which cross references the user roles and functions. Critical dialogues are identified, and service levels defined for all functions.

STEP 340   ENHANCE REQUIRED DATA MODEL

The Logical Data Model has been derived from the top down, and structured to ensure support for the processing shown in the Required System Data Flow Model. This may not be the most efficient structure, so Relational Data Analysis is now applied to groups of data items to put them into at least Third Normal Form (TNF). The steps to do this are:

  − Remove any repeating groups to put the data into First Normal Form.

  − Ensure that all data items are dependent on the key. The data is then in Second Normal Form.

  − Ensure that all items other than the key are independent of each other. The data is then in Third Normal Form.

Data in Third Normal Form is therefore a grouping of items in which:

  − there are no repeating groups;

  − all the data items are functionally dependent on the key and independent of each other;

Normalisation is an automatic but time-consuming task, so it is not carried out on all the Input/Output Structures. The ones selected are based on their complexity, volume, frequency and importance.

When the chosen data structures have been normalised, they are set out as an LDS type of diagram. This is then compared with the Required System Logical Data Structure, and differences are considered and resolved.

STEP 350 DEVELOP SPECIFICATION PROTOTYPES

This step is optional, the boundaries and objectives of the prototyping exercise being defined by the project board.

There are various types and different approaches to prototyping. It is not the intention to build the system from the prototypes in an incremental way. It is used here with the purpose of identifying errors and misunderstandings that have remained hidden until now, and as an aid to the development of menus and command structures.

Prototyping is done on a selection of dialogues and report formats. The exercise will have served its purpose when the menus and command structures have been agreed with the users, and any changes incorporated into the Requirements Catalogue and Requirements Specification. Dialogues and report formats not considered here will be dealt with at Step 510.

STEP 360 DEVELOP PROCESSING SPECIFICATION

Step 360 requires very detailed consideration of the processing to be carried out in the required system. Data Flow Diagrams show the processing without regard to sequence or priority. These attributes are now decided during the construction of the Entity Life Histories. It can be expected that this exercise will reveal a significant number of omissions from the DFDs. This is not a reflection on the effort that has been put into the development of the DFDs, but a consequence of looking at requirements from a different viewpoint.

The process is carried out by working up from the bottom of the Logical Data Structure to create the ELHs for the normal lives of the entities. The procedure is then reversed, working from the top down to add the abnormalities, and to consider the events that also affect other entities.

A single event can have several effects, and can affect more than one entity. The totality of these effects are shown on Effect Correspondence Diagrams, with one for each event. Construction of these may lead to changes in the Requirements Catalogue and the Logical Data Model. Specifically, volumetric information is added to the LDS.

Work on the ELHs relates to updates, ie things happening to the data to change its state. Processing relating to enquiries is now covered by the creation of Enquiry Access Paths, with one for each enquiry.

STEP 370 CONFIRM SYSTEM OBJECTIVES

This step provides a final review of requirements before considering their implementation in Stage 4. Up to this point, entries have been made in the

Requirements Catalogue as the need for them has been identified. The objective of the review is to ensure that all requirements have been identified and fully defined. The Requirements Catalogue is considered in conjunction with the Function Definitions and the Required System Logical Data Model.

It is important to ensure that the non-functional requirements of resources and qualities (how much and how well) are specified in a measurable form. Without this, performance will be down to the discretion of the designers or, regrettably, to pot luck. Users cannot hope to get the performance they need unless they have said what it is. It is likely to cause extra costs if the right levels of performance are not built into the initial design. Provided that performance objectives have been agreed, users are reasonably entitled to reject a system that fails to meet them.

STEP 380   ASSEMBLE REQUIREMENTS SPECIFICATION

Step 380 completes the work of Stage 3. All the documentation is reviewed. Products are cross-checked and assembled into the Requirements Specification. The Requirements Specification comprises:

- Data Catalogue, containing:

  • Attribute/Data Item Descriptions;

  • Grouped Domain Descriptions.

- Requirements Catalogue.

- Processing Specification, consisting of:

  • User Role/Function Matrix;

  • Function Definitions, containing:

      Function Definitions,

      I/O Structures,

      Enquiry Access Paths,

      (Common) Elementary Process Descriptions.

  • Required System LDM, consisting of:

      LDS,

      Entity Descriptions,

      Relationship Descriptions,

  • Entity Life Histories;

  • Effect Correspondence Diagrams.

16

Stage 4 – Technical System Options

INTRODUCTION

A Business System Option was chosen in Stage 2, and the requirements were then comprehensively analysed in Stage 3. This gave a Requirements Specification that set out the requirements as agreed by management, the business areas concerned, and the computer department. At this point the requirements are precisely known, but the actual implementation will present a further range of choices. Examples are:

- in-house   v   bought-in development;

- package   v   customised solution;

- 4GL   v   procedural language;

- centralised   v   distributed;

- mainframe   v   micros;

- conventional files v   database;

- evolution   v   'big bang'.

- some combination of these or other possibilities.

The choice is made in Stage 4. It is similar to Stage 2 (Business System Options) in approach (*see* Figure 16.1). Several possibilities are considered, perhaps three are developed in more detail, then one is chosen.

STEP 410   DEFINE TECHNICAL SYSTEM OPTIONS

Step 410 mirrors Step 210. The system constraints that all options must meet are identified. Then up to six Technical Systems Options are defined. They are

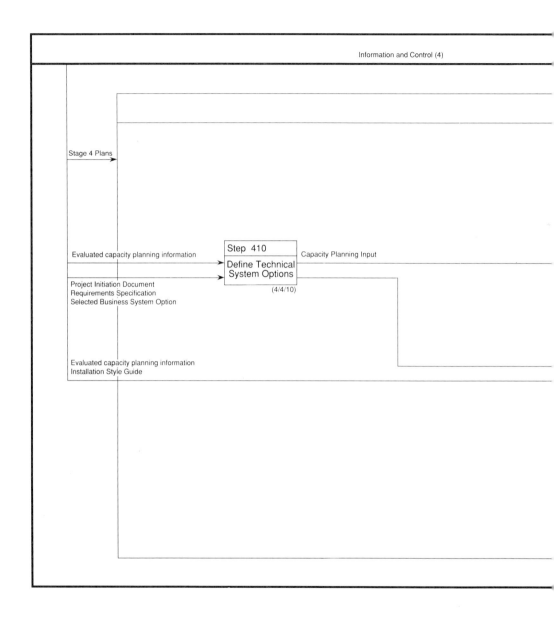

Figure 16.1 Stage 4

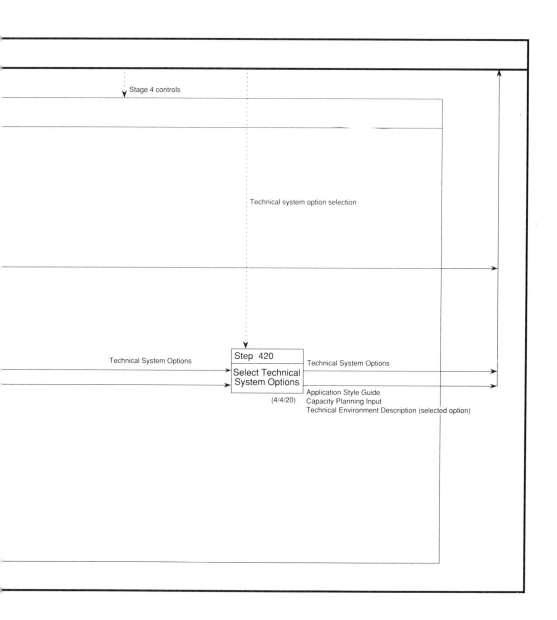

discussed with users and two or three options are short-listed. A description of each short-listed option is developed, comprising:

- Technical Environment Description.

- System Description.

- Capacity planning information for each option.

- Impact Analysis.

- Outline Development Plan.

- Cost Benefit Analysis.

STEP 420   SELECT TECHNICAL SYSTEM OPTION

The Technical System Options developed at Step 410 are presented to the project board and one (or a hybrid) is selected. As for the Business System Option, the selection is a business decision to be taken by the sponsors of the project. The documentation is updated to describe the choice made. The chosen option must be capable of achieving the quantitative targets that have been set.

17
Stage 5 – Logical Design

INTRODUCTION

Stage 5, shown at Figure 17.1, completes the logical design of the system. It is subdivided into three parts:

- Dialogue Design.

- Update Process Design.

- Enquiry Process Design.

In Step 420 a specific technical solution was agreed. However, the specification created in Stage 5 is one that can be implemented independently of the technical environment.

STEP 510   DEFINE USER DIALOGUES

The User Role/Function Matrix identifies what dialogues are required. Step 510 deals with the logical aspects of dialogue design, ie the structure of each dialogue, and the relationships between different dialogues. It is therefore interested in the logical groupings of dialogue elements, and these are documented in Dialogue Control Tables. Other details to be considered are the menu structure and help facilities.

STEP 520   DEFINE UPDATE PROCESSES

All updates result from events that are shown on the Entity Life Histories. The diagrams show the events in the sequence in which they occur. The processing checks must ensure that this sequence is obeyed, so the sequential information contained in the diagrams must be transferred to the processing specifications. The first step is to add state indicators to the ELHs.

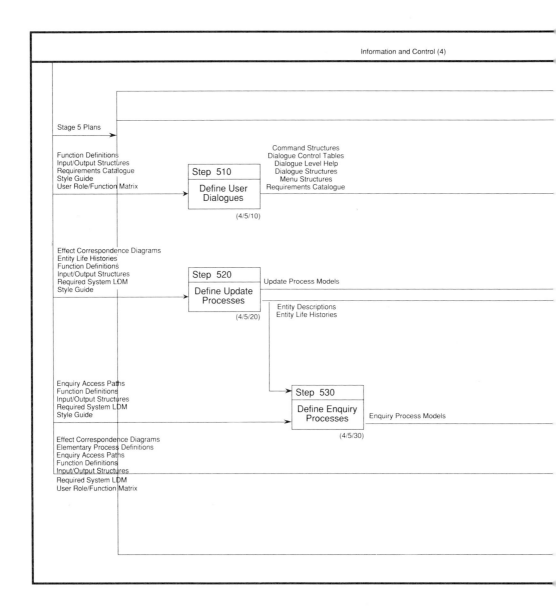

Information and Control (4)

Stage 5 Plans

Function Definitions
Input/Output Structures
Requirements Catalogue
Style Guide
User Role/Function Matrix

Command Structures
Dialogue Control Tables
Dialogue Level Help
Dialogue Structures
Menu Structures
Requirements Catalogue

Step 510

Define User
Dialogues

(4/5/10)

Effect Correspondence Diagrams
Entity Life Histories
Function Definitions
Input/Output Structures
Required System LDM
Style Guide

Step 520

Define Update
Processes

(4/5/20)

Update Process Models

Entity Descriptions
Entity Life Histories

Enquiry Access Paths
Function Definitions
Input/Output Structures
Required System LDM
Style Guide

Step 530

Define Enquiry
Processes

(4/5/30)

Enquiry Process Models

Effect Correspondence Diagrams
Elementary Process Definitions
Enquiry Access Paths
Function Definitions
Input/Output Structures
Required System LDM
User Role/Function Matrix

Figure 17.1 Stage 5

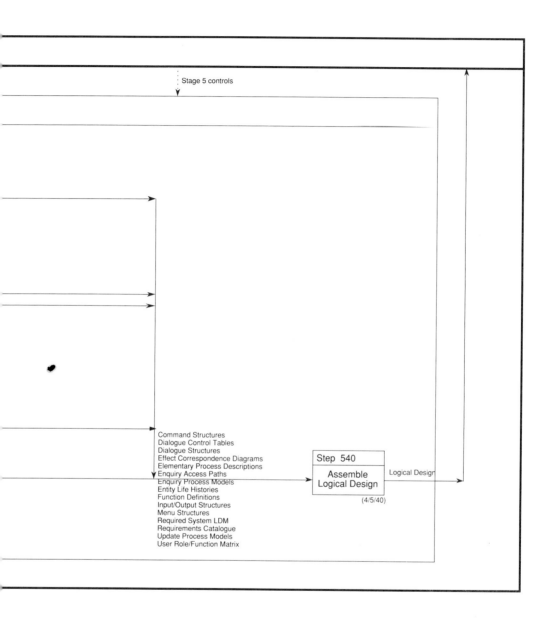

Stage 5 controls

Command Structures
Dialogue Control Tables
Dialogue Structures
Effect Correspondence Diagrams
Elementary Process Descriptions
Enquiry Access Paths
Enquiry Process Models
Entity Life Histories
Function Definitions
Input/Output Structures
Menu Structures
Required System LDM
Requirements Catalogue
Update Process Models
User Role/Function Matrix

Step 540

Assemble
Logical Design

(4/5/40)

Logical Design

The Effect Correspondence Diagrams are converted into processing structures. Operations, derived from the ELHs and including the state indicator checks, are listed and added to the process structures. Conditions governing selection and iteration are then added, and error outputs specified.

STEP 530 DEFINE ENQUIRY PROCESSES

Enquiries include those operations that are purely enquiries, and also the enquiry elements of updating operations. For each enquiry, the Enquiry Access Paths are converted into processing structures that represent input data structures.

Output data structures are created from the Input/Output Structures. For each enquiry, the input and output structures are merged to give one processing structure. Operations and conditions governing selection and iteration are added to the structure, and error outputs are specified.

STEP 540 ASSEMBLE LOGICAL DESIGN

The final step in Stage 5 consists of a review of the logical design products for completeness and consistency. The documentation is then assembled as the Logical Design, which comprises:

- Logical Process Model; which contains:

  - Dialogues;

  - Effect Correspondence Diagrams;

  - Enquiry Process Models;

  - Function Definitions;

  - Update Process Models.

- Menu Structures

- Command Structures

- Requirements Catalogue

- Data Catalogue; containing:

  - Attribute/Data Item Descriptions,

  - Domain Descriptions.

- Required System LDM; consisting of:

  - LDS,

  - Entity Descriptions;

  - Relationship Descriptions.

18
Stage 6 – Physical Design

INTRODUCTION

Physical design is encompassed in Stage 6. The logical design created in Stage 5 is converted into the physical design envisaged by the selected Technical System Option. It consists of seven steps. The output is the Physical Design, which goes forward to the production stage of the development cycle.

STEP 610   PREPARE FOR PHYSICAL DESIGN

This step draws up the plans and makes the rules for the rest of the work in Stage 6. It takes stock of the facilities provided by the tools that are to be used for development, by classifying the facilities they provide against parameters regarding processing, storage and performance.

Standards are established for:

- use of the physical processing system;

- data base management system (DBMS) facilities;

- data design rules;

- names;

- program specification.

An Activity Network and Activity Descriptions are prepared to cover the work of the remaining steps in physical design.

A start is made on the preparation of user, operation and training manuals. The plans are agreed with the project board.

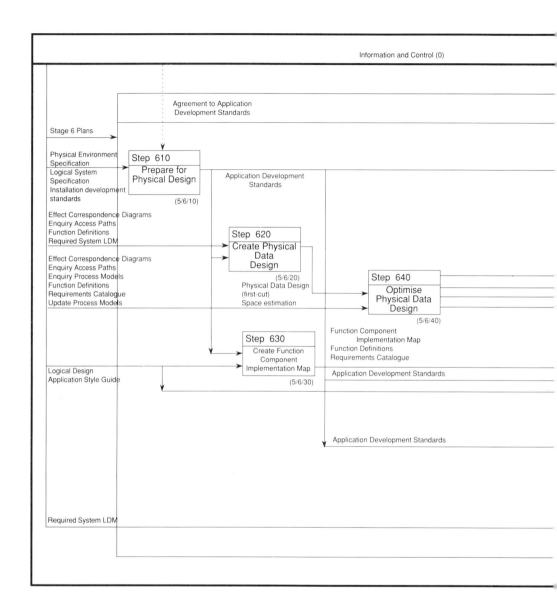

Information and Control (0)

Agreement to Application
Development Standards

Stage 6 Plans

Physical Environment
Specification
Logical System
Specification
Installation development
standards

Step 610
Prepare for
Physical Design

(5/6/10)

Application Development
Standards

Effect Correspondence Diagrams
Enquiry Access Paths
Function Definitions
Required System LDM

Effect Correspondence Diagrams
Enquiry Access Paths
Enquiry Process Models
Function Definitions
Requirements Catalogue
Update Process Models

Step 620
Create Physical
Data
Design

(5/6/20)
Physical Data Design
(first-cut)
Space estimation

Step 640
Optimise
Physical Data
Design

(5/6/40)

Function Component
Implementation Map
Function Definitions
Requirements Catalogue

Step 630
Create Function
Component
Implementation Map

(5/6/30)

Logical Design
Application Style Guide

Application Development Standards

Application Development Standards

Required System LDM

© Crown Copyright July 1990 – SSADM Version 4

Figure 18.1 Stage 6

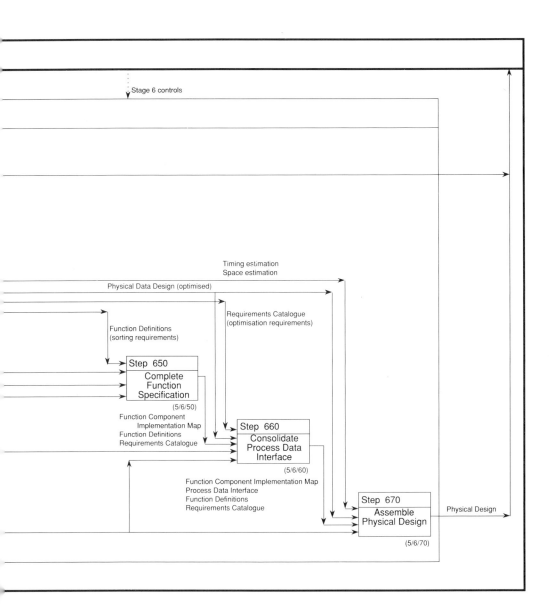

STEP 620   CREATE PHYSICAL DATA DESIGN

In Step 620 the Required System Logical Data Model is converted into a physical design. This is a first-cut design, ie a legitimate design that would run in the chosen DBMS. It would not give the optimum performance. At this point it may well not even give an adequate performance. Performance targets are considered at Step 640.

STEP 630   CREATE FUNCTION COMPONENT IMPLEMENTATION MAP

The Logical Design produced during Stage 5 covers all the processing required by the users. It is now given further consideration. Processing may now need to be defined for:

- syntax error handling;

- controls and control error handling;

- physical input and output formats.

There may be duplication and common processing.

System failure must be considered. In the event of failure, some transactions may be only part processed. The dangers are:

- a process that has only been part actioned at system failure may be fully repeated when processing is resumed, thus leading to duplicate updating of some files;

- a process that has been part completed may be left incomplete, with some updates missing.

In either case, the data will be wrong. Units of processing that must be fully complete are known as success units. Procedures are needed to ensure the correct and full processing of each success unit, and hence the integrity of the data, when processing is resumed.

Development tools may permit some of the processing to be specified non-procedurally (ie specified by defining *what* must be done rather than *how* to do it). This should be done now. Processes defined procedurally are dealt with at Step 650. Database access components are specified at Step 660.

STEP 640   OPTIMISE PHYSICAL DATA DESIGN

The physical data design, when implemented, must achieve the targets set out in the Requirements Catalogue. These relate to the space taken up by the data, and the time taken to carry out the processing. The first-cut physical data design created at Step 620 may not meet these objectives. Step 640 is concerned with achieving them. To this end, the data design may need some modification to make it more compact, or able to respond to the processing more efficiently. Failure to achieve the objectives at this late stage could prove costly. Likely consequences are:

- the purchase of more hardware;

- fundamental rethinking of the design;

- reassessment of the objectives themselves;

- abandonment of the project.

None of these consequences will enhance the reputation of the computer department. The possibility that any of these could happen is an excellent reason for not skimping on any of the comprehensive checking that is specified as needing to be carried out in all the earlier stages of SSADM.

STEP 650   COMPLETE FUNCTION SPECIFICATION

Functions that could be described non-procedurally were actioned at Step 630. Step 650 now deals with the specification and design of the procedural components. These procedural specifications provide the detail required by the programmers. Logical processes are combined into physical programs or run-units.

Database access components are dealt with at Step 660.

STEP 660   CONSOLIDATE PROCESS DATA INTERFACE

In this step a comparison is made between the actual physical design and the Required System Logical Data Model from which it has been developed. Mismatches are investigated. The whole design is considered for:

- effective use of development software;

- ease of implementing future changes, both to requirements and to the physical environment;

- components which fail to fully meet the requirements.

STEP 670   ASSEMBLE PHYSICAL DESIGN

The final step in SSADM is concerned with a review of the products of Stage 6 for completeness and consistency. The documents are then assembled as the Physical Design.

Part 4

Implementing SSADM

Considerations for Management

19

Implementing SSADM – an introduction

INTRODUCTION

Taking on SSADM will change the way the work is done. More effort is put into analysis, which inevitably delays the start of subsequent work. Managers who fear that no real progress is being made until programming is under way will be worried. It requires an act of faith to believe that there will be savings later, on program design, coding, testing, implementation, maintenance, and user satisfaction.

CONSIDERATIONS

SSADM has the potential to solve many problems of systems development, but there are provisos:

- It does not guarantee that the right systems will be developed. That is a matter of strategic judgement for company management.

- It is not a panacea. Its use will not automatically guarantee better systems. Nor is it aimed at the development of systems other than for data processing. However, for data processing systems it is very effective.

- Whilst it is freely available, assimilating the method will take time, even for an experienced analyst. Training is going to be needed to get the best out of it. Initially, practitioners:

  • may have difficulty with the techniques;

  • will not fully understand why they are doing what they are doing;

  • will not appreciate how it all fits together.

- Much of the early-day struggles with the method can be avoided by the judicious employment of experienced consultants. This has a cost, although their employment does not necessarily have to be for long periods. Short visits at strategic points in the application of the method can be very effective.

- The close involvement of knowledgeable users is critical to the successful development of the system (as it is with any method).

- The potential gains of high quality development may be lost if similarly good methods are not used throughout the remaining stages of development.

PREVIEW OF PART 4

The remaining chapters in this part consider some of the subjects that will require the attention of any organisation that plans to start using SSADM.

Quality assurance is essential to the success of the method. SSADM does not specify how to go about it, on the assumption that it is a fundamental task that is already being carried out. Chapter 20 is for those organisations for which this is a false assumption. Most of the points raised in Chapter 20 will apply equally to any method.

System development failures when using SSADM can be due to many factors, some of which are:

- inexperience;

- lack of training;

- bloody mindedness by practitioners over the use of a new method;

- lack of effective user involvement;

- lack of control.

These are problems for management, the first four of which require general management skills and commitment to resolve. Chapter 21 is about the last of these – project management. SSADM is not a substitute for management. It does not manage itself, but it does provide all that is necessary for effective management. As with QA, many of the points raised are general ones, but are critical for the success of a project. It is all too easy to blame SSADM for a failure when the real failure was lack of control.

An SSADM development is very detailed and thorough. The investigation does not miss very much. A lot of information is collected and recorded, with consequent demands on paper and an effective filing system. Alternatively a CASE (Computer Aided Software Engineering) tool can be employed, but this has purchasing costs and learning delays. These tools can vary considerably in the level of help they provide and may not support all the work entailed in SSADM. Some points to consider before investing in a CASE tool are mentioned in Chapter 22.

Finally, in Chapter 23, some practical suggestions are made for those who decide to go ahead with the introduction of SSADM. If followed, these suggestions should help towards the successful development of the first project. This will in turn lead to the general acceptance of the method, and its use for further projects. The payoff will be seen in systems that are more robust and do more of what users need.

20

Quality Assurance — QA

INTRODUCTION

THE NEED FOR Q Control

As a system investigation proceeds, all the information will be set down as it is gathered. Unfortunately, that does not mean that what is set down will be correct. There will be misunderstandings and mistakes. If these are not picked up, then they will be built into the system.

It has long been known that design errors and omissions that remain undiscovered until testing or after implementation may cost 100 times as much to correct compared with the cost of errors found before moving on from design (*Boehm,* 1976). Certainly the cost can be out of all proportion to the apparent triviality of the problem. Any effort spent trying to pick up these errors and omissions can be regarded as an investment.

Quality assurance (QA) is an integral part of SSADM (and unless the quality attained by SSADM is to be put at risk, it should also be applied throughout every subsequent aspect of system development). How the work is done is left to individual organisations. The Inspection approach described here is not a part of SSADM, but is a procedure applicable at any time, with any method.

QA is concerned with ensuring that:

— the method is being used correctly;

— the specified products are available;

— the products are complete in themselves and are cross-checked against other products;

— the work conforms to installation standards;

— the system will do, functionally, what it is supposed to do;

- the required levels of design objectives are achievable, ie how well the system is to perform, as distinct from what it must do.

LEVELS OF QA

QA procedures can be considered at four levels:

- Informal, for products that do not go forward from the end of a step, either because they are development documents leading to a final document that will be subject to a formal review, or because they are internal to a step.

- Formal, ie a checkpoint that involves the setting up of a meeting that is subject to documentation and rework.

- Project board assessment, where the current state of development is considered in all its aspects and implications for the organisation. This is done at the end of each module, but may be needed at other times if it becomes apparent that the planned targets will not be achieved.

- Project board authorisation, when the work done is accepted (with or without comments/recommendations) and approval is given to continue with the next module.

QA PROCEDURES

QA can be conducted in various ways. Many organisations have their own procedures that may be applied to the SSADM products. Government computing uses procedures laid down in the PRINCE Project Management Method. Another commonly used approach is the Structured Walkthrough, although the practice is variable.

The method that has been shown to give the best results is the Inspection Method, pioneered by Michael Fagan of IBM. Reported results suggest that Inspections can find 70–80 percent of design and coding errors. A comparative test with a structured walkthrough showed that the Inspection sample contained 38 percent fewer errors (*Fagan*, 1976).

The Inspection Method is described briefly below.

THE INSPECTION METHOD

Inspection is an attempt to introduce the disciplines of engineering into software development. Its objective (in common with other approaches) is to detect errors as soon as possible in the project life cycle. It can take place after any control point in the development process has been reached. This will normally be the availability of a product on completion of a task. As a separate Inspection of each product would often be impractical, some grouping is necessary in practice, and depends on the volume of work and the interval since the last Inspection.

Basically, Inspection is a comparison method. It tries to find differences between the product of work carried out at one level and the product of the previous level. Ultimately the aim is to confirm that the two are exactly equivalent. A product cannot be used as the basis for further development until an Inspection has been satisfactorily completed. Rigorous rules are laid down as to what should be examined, when this should be, and against what criteria.

Inspection principles

- Inspections are carried out at prescribed checkpoints throughout the development life cycle. Major ones are set by the project board; others by the project manager.

- The Inspection is for all defects, for example, logic, function, use of the method, adherence to standards, achievement of specified levels of performance, development staying under control and within estimates.

- Inspection is by colleagues at all levels of seniority, preferably from different teams (the documentation should be self-explanatory). Ideally a meeting should involve from three to five people including a Moderator. Exceptionally there may be more, if each has something unique to offer.

- Inspections are carried out in a prescribed way (*see* Inspection Practice).

- Inspections are led by the Moderator. Ideally, the Moderator should be trained, but training often consists of learning by experience. The Moderator is responsible for the administrative arrangements, leading the meeting, noting and classifying the defects, arranging follow-up action, and checking that it has been done.

- Checklists are used, featuring checks that should be made, and paying particular attention to areas that have been particularly error-prone on previous Inspections. Quality checklists are provided in the Product Descriptions section of the *SSADM Version 4 Reference Manual*. The lessons learned on each development should be carried forward into future projects.

- Inspectors have specialist roles, each of which should have its own checklist. In the absence of formal training, such lists should be built up in the light of experience of Inspections within the organisation.

- Meetings are limited to two hours (which may mean that more than one meeting is needed to cover all the material).

- Inspections must be driven at the optimum rate. This will vary between different installations and different teams. Going too slowly wastes time. Going too quickly may mean that errors are missed, and this is likely to be much more time-consuming in the long term.

- Statistics of defects are maintained and analysed. These are used to identify areas of weakness that could be improved, to measure the effectiveness of the Inspection process, and as feedback to improve future Inspections.

Inspection Practice

- Planning is done by the Moderator, who decides who to involve, and when and where to hold the meeting.

- An overview is optional, depending on the existing knowledge of the Inspection team. It would be omitted when the team are familiar with the project.

- Preparation is done individually by the Inspectors from the circulated documentation. They are expected to spend about one and a half hours familiarising themselves with the material and identifying possible defects before the meeting. It is important that this is done, and time should be scheduled for it. THIS ALSO DEPEND ON HOW big IS THE PROJECT.

- At the meeting itself, all suspected defects are identified by the Inspectors and recorded by the Moderator. No attempt is made to provide solutions.

- After the meeting, the Moderator arranges for rework to clear the suspected defects. Some may be nothing more than ambiguous documentation, but ambiguity is itself a fault that must be rectified.

- It is the responsibility of the Moderator to ensure that follow up action has been taken to rework all defects.

- As discussion of solutions is not permitted during the Inspection meeting, a Third Hour Meeting may be held (optionally) when Inspectors can go beyond the identification of defects and can discuss any ideas they may have.

References

More information on Inspections can be found in *Fagan* (1976), and *Gilb,* (1988).

QA and SSADM

Apart from the formal end of stage reviews, the formality and frequency of other reviews are matters for managerial judgement, bearing in mind that reviews take time, but not so much as building on work that is eventually found to have been defective.

The basic principles are:

- All documents created since the last review must be reviewed for a first time.

- All documents changed since the last review must be reviewed again.

- All references on all forms and diagrams must be checked for accuracy and relevance.

- Some documents that have not been changed will also need review, where they could have been affected by changes made elsewhere.

- The end of a step provides a logical review point.

- The size of the system will have a direct bearing on the frequency of the reviews. For a small system it may be sensible to group together more than one formal review. For a large system, it may be advisable to carry out some reviews at task or even at product level. The main criterion is the amount of work done since the last review, and the optimum time of two hours for a review meeting.

MAINTAINING QUALITY AFTER SSADM

The work done during the competent application of SSADM will have resulted in a well-structured system design, from which an equally well-structured system can be built. However, without the use of effective program design techniques, continued quality assurance procedures, and well-planned tests, it is still possible to destroy both design quality and credibility with the user. The Inspection principles must be applied throughout the remainder of development.

21
Project Management

INTRODUCTION

This chapter considers project management in relation to the area of development covered by SSADM, and also introduces some other important but more general points. Many installations will have their own methods of project management. Within central government the approved project management standard is PRINCE. Those who would like to implement the NCC approach should refer to the *Project Management and Control Manual* (NCC Publications 1988).

THE NEED FOR PROJECT MANAGEMENT

If a computer system is to satisfy the anticipated cost/benefit estimates and to be welcomed by the user, it must be brought in:

- within time;

- within cost;

- doing what the user needs.

The chances of satisfying time, cost and needs without control are remote. Project management aims to provide this control. Unfortunately the reality is that all too often these criteria of successful development are not achieved even with a control method. A standard development method is also needed, and SSADM gives this. It provides the following aids to the effective management of projects:

- the same approach to every project, which permits the building up of a statistical base to improve the estimating process;

- the Module/Stage/Step/Task structure, which gives the basis for estimating and monitoring progress;

125

    – the products, which provide the basis for reporting progress

Remember that project management activities must themselves feature in a project management system, ie they:

    – take time;

    – cost money.

    These resources must be used effectively. It is possible to spend large amounts of time making returns, collating figures, drawing graphs, updating schedules, etc. Project management is a means to an end, not an end in itself.

Time Wasters

Before proceeding to project management activities, it is worth considering how time can be wasted during an SSADM development. These misuses of development time should be guarded against or resolved as soon as possible. Immense amounts of time can be spent on:

    – Failing to establish the initial scope of the study (allowing work to be done that will be irrelevant to the system as eventually agreed).

    – Permitting detailed work to be done on elements of the system that are beyond the agreed scope (interesting diversions no doubt, and quite possibly of value in the future, but of no real use to the work in hand).

    – Permitting the redrawing of diagrams to the point where they become works of art or draughtsmanship rather than working documents. Diagrams are adequate if they are understandable, except perhaps for the formal QA reviews and final documentation.

    – Allowing iteration to continue unchecked, within or between tasks, in the search for the totally complete specification.

    – Failing to organise people to be available at the appropriate times for interviews, meetings, and reviews (the alternatives being either waiting for people, or the potentially even greater time waster of making decisions without consultation).

    Experience has shown that these time wasters can easily double the cost and timescale of a project with no increase in benefits. Good project management must be constantly on guard against such irrelevancies.

Avoiding Problems

If the work is to be done within schedule it is essential that:

    – Any potential growth in the content of the system is identified and notified to management *before* extra work is done.

- Any slippage is identified and corrected as it occurs. There is a frequent hope, seldom realised, that time lost during a project can be made up at the end. This is often attempted in a 'traditional' development environment by omitting the documentation and skimping on testing. Documentation cannot be omitted in SSADM as each task depends on earlier documentation. Being less than thorough with testing leaves errors and omissions to be found after implementation, and this causes:

  • annoyance and inconvenience to users;

  • financial loss to the organisation;

  • loss of credibility for the computer department.

  In any event, the price will be paid later.

- If as a project proceeds it begins to get behind schedule there comes a point, often fairly early, when no amount of extra resources will bring it back on schedule. The effort of training people and the increase in lines of communication may become counter-productive.

- The technical staff must not take it upon themselves to build in extra facilities that they think would be useful. No changes should be made without considering their effect on time and cost, and without obtaining the necessary level of agreement before starting. Development staff must *not* do what may well seem to them to be the common sense thing. Initially they must persuade the project manager of the need for the change and for any consequential additional work. Then, before it is done, the user must be consulted before the changes are made, or before either timescale or cost is increased in any way. Failure to do so could prove to be very expensive for the developers. In extreme cases this could result in the rejection of the system. (*See* section on Change Control).

- The developers must not diverge in any way from their scheduled tasks without first checking with the project manager. Programmers have been known to become consumed by the technical challenges. The effort required to save a couple of hundred bytes or to save a few microseconds is not worth the effort as a technical exercise. It can only be justified if the saving is essential for storage or performance purposes. Similarly the convoluted logic of a development genius can take an extraordinary amount of time for lesser mortals to understand subsequently.

- Any potential difficulties, problems or delays should be reported for consideration at the earliest possible moment, whilst it is still possible for the project manager to do something about it.

ELEMENTS OF PROJECT MANAGEMENT

Project management is not an integral part of SSADM, but is essential for the success of an SSADM project (and any other project). It consists of a range of activities:

- Planning:

  - estimation;

  - scheduling;

  - evaluation;

- Authorisation.

- Monitoring, of

  - progress against time and cost budgets;

  - quality;

  - user involvement.

- Change Control.

- Rescheduling.

- Document Control.

- Collection of statistics.

These activities are considered in more detail in the sections that follow.

ESTIMATION

The Problems

As work proceeds on any system, more is known and less remains to be done. It is possible, and usually essential, to refine estimates regularly as work proceeds, and this is done in SSADM. Even so it can still be difficult, in what is theoretically the last week of a project, to be sure that nothing will be carried forward into the following week.

If estimating when near the end of a project cannot be done with total confidence, then early estimates are obviously much more prone to error. Estimation in the early stages of system development is a classic example of the Catch 22 situation − an estimate cannot be made with any great hope of ultimately being proved correct by events until the work involved is known in considerable detail. On the other hand, management is understandably reluctant to sanction work to go ahead to this level of detail in the absence of some estimate of what the costs are likely to be.

The figure that tends to stick in the minds of users/senior management is the one they were first given, and this is almost invariably lower than actual cost. Projects all too often exceed their early estimates by 100 percent or more. The detail needed for any sort of accuracy in estimating is missing until the requirements have been fully identified. Regrettably, this is often a little late to be producing estimates that would show that the project should not have been started in the first place. There is always the temptation to continue with a project once a significant amount of money has been spent on it, even though the cost/benefit calculations, when reconsidered, would show a totally different picture. Management must be prepared to stop a project if that is the best decision for the business. (Revision of estimates is considered further under *Monitoring with SSADM).*

The first problem is that of producing time and cost estimates during the Feasibility Study that will bear some acceptably close resemblance to actual subsequent experience. At the same time, users/management must be made aware of the degree of error that is likely in these early estimates, and the basis on which they have been made.

Estimating is not easy. There are many approaches, all eminently capable of producing figures that are well wide of the mark. Unfortunately there is no infallible tool that will give an accurate estimate, or anything near to it, without considerable effort on the part of those making the estimate. Consider just some of the many factors involved:

- type of project;

- complexity of system;

- team organisation;

- experience of team;

- methods used;

- availability of equipment;

- availability of software.

and so on.

Other factors that are also needed are:

- sufficient statistics of past performance in identical circumstances on which to base the estimates;

- major features of the proposed system known in reasonable detail;

- no changes to requirements to be actioned during development without prior re-estimation.

If all of these and any other relevant items are taken into account, then there is hope of producing estimates that bear some resemblance to the subsequent reality. Being pinned to a hopelessly optimistic estimate is a situation that ultimately gives satisfaction to no-one. The development staff may then choose to take all sorts of short cuts, making decisions that should really be made by users, and being less than thorough with testing. This destroys much that has been gained by the use of a structured method. Targets must be realistic.

Making Estimates

Estimates can be made in several ways:

- by calculation (*Boehm 1981, Putnam 1980*);

- by Function Points (*Albrecht* and *Gaffney 1983, Behrens 1983*);

- by breaking the development process down into its constituent parts and estimating for each of them separately.

Estimating is not only a management task. Involving members of the team in estimating can prevent some of the initial over-optimism, and is more likely to lead to acceptance, commitment and motivation of the team.

The basis of each element of the estimate should be recorded, so that future estimates can be refined in the light of experience.

Software is available that can help with the task of estimating. Such packages are built on statistical bases derived (inevitably in the first instance) from experience in other organisations. They can thus be taken as a guide, but require customisation from statistics that are installation-specific. Inevitably this takes some time and effort.

Estimating and SSADM

A work breakdown is readily available from the SSADM tasks, customised as necessary, and giving clearly defined start and end points in terms of inputs and products. (These must be augmented by estimates of the non-SSADM work that must also be done.) Estimates on this basis are also needed for scheduling purposes. It is sensible to have an estimate by an alternative approach for purposes of comparison. Any significant discrepancy between the two estimates would serve as a warning, and would clearly indicate the need for some further thought.

Estimates are drawn up, reviewed, authorised, monitored against actual performance, and revised as necessary.

In SSADM, estimates are included in the Module Plans for approval by the project board.

SCHEDULING

Purpose

The purpose of scheduling is to take the estimated resource requirements for each activity, together with the known resource availability. Then, allowing for the logical interrelationships of activities, it is possible to establish start and end dates for each of them.

Bases for scheduling

Scheduling may be done in one of two ways:

- By allocating available resources to the tasks, to decide how long the project will take;

- By taking the time available and deciding what resources are necessary to meet the target dates (remembering that the target may be impossible; if it would take a five man team an estimated 40 weeks to complete (a total of 200 man weeks) then 200 people could not complete it in a week, and it is unlikely that 20 people could do it in 10 weeks).

Uncertainties

It is important to beware of dependence on external factors, for example:

- deliveries of hardware;

- performance of new equipment and software.

Late deliveries or failure to perform can have a dramatic effect on plans, and the possibility of this happening must be considered when formulating the plan. Items which are particularly vulnerable to delay are those that do not yet exist. Delivery of any item that is under development by a supplier must be open to doubt. He may run into problems, or his priorities might change.

All other areas of uncertainty should be identified so that particular attention can be paid to them. They will include such items as:

- searching for anything, eg suitable software;

- gaining effective practical experience after receiving training;

- communicating between different items of equipment for the first time.

The scheduling process

Scheduling is done by matching the resources known to be available to the customised SSADM tasks, to which the estimates have been assigned.

From the SSADM task estimates, a further breakdown may be required so that each activity:

- has a clear boundary with defined inputs and products;

- can be performed by a single individual or a small team;

- will last for only a short period - ideally no more than two weeks;

- must include user involvement in detail.

In establishing the relationships between the various activities it will be necessary to identify:

- activities which must be performed in sequence;

- activities which can take place in parallel.

The relationships are best shown diagrammatically on a network analysis diagram, for example, Critical Path Analysis or PERT (Programme Evaluation and Review Technique), which permit identification of the critical path. The act of drawing up such a network is itself a check on the completeness of the analysis, and usually reveals omissions.

In preparing schedules, factors to be considered are:

- known absences, eg training courses, meetings, presentations, seminars, vacations, Bank Holidays, etc (for practical purposes it may be wise to assume that no progress will be made for two weeks at Christmas, and very little in August; whatever the good intentions, there is major disruption during these periods);

- an allowance for the possibility of absence due to sickness;

- training of new staff due to turnover or promotion;

- the intrusion of non-project activities;

- contributions of team members to the planning process;

- involvement of team members in quality assurance;

- turnround time for compilations and tests;

- the management element;

- allowances for uncertainties (contingency time).

A fairly common practice is to assume a three and a half or four day week for estimating purposes.

When activities have been assigned to people (with or without a network diagram) they can be entered on a bar chart.

Contingency and management time

The term *Contingency,* as used here, is an allowance for the uncertainties that are inherent in any system development. It is additional to the basic resource estimates for the expected work content of a project, and may be defined as a reserve resource that must be carefully controlled. Some organisations may wish to delegate different percentages of the total allowance for contingency to different levels of control.

Both contingency and management time must be considered as separate elements when making estimates, ie they should not be built into the estimates for individual tasks.

Multiple projects

Where an individual is working on more than one project, the demands of each must be taken into account on the schedules. This may require a separate staff schedule for the individual. An allowance must also be made for 'lost time' due to continually switching between projects.

Software aids

All but the simplest schedules are difficult to modify or maintain on paper, and the use of software should be considered.

Many software packages are available. Features for consideration include:

- How many activities does it support?

- How many resources are allowed?

- Does it draw network diagrams?

- Does it produce bar charts?

- What output devices can be used?

- Does it give resource levelling/smoothing?

- How does it deal with rescheduling?

More general features that should be considered are mentioned in Chapter 23 in the consideration of CASE tools.

EVALUATION

When the scheduling has been completed, the project delivery time and cost must be reviewed. If there is any indication that either of them is likely to exceed the resource objectives, then further high level consideration will be required. Options for management are one or more of the following:

- accepting a smaller system by redrawing the system boundary;

- accepting a simpler system by omitting some of the requirements;

- accepting a simpler system by requiring fewer of the problems to be solved;

- relaxing some of the design objectives to accept a lower level of performance;

- accepting an increase in time and cost.

Short cuts through SSADM should not be taken. This would cause a loss in the quality of the product. The apparent saving of analysis and design time would be a short term saving, with greater costs in the later stages of development, user acceptance and subsequent maintenance.

AUTHORISATION

The Project Plans and all Module Plans require authorisation from the project board before work can continue.

MONITORING

Purpose

The purpose of monitoring is to:

- check that work is proceeding according to plan, ie by both developers and users, within time and cost;

- ensure that work is aimed at achieving the required levels of performance specified in the design objectives;

- ensure that the work is being done to SSADM and installation stand-ards;

- take corrective action where appropriate;

- reschedule the work when necessary.

Monitoring with SSADM

SSADM aids monitoring by virtue of the prescribed tasks which break the project down into small units of work with end products for each step. Monitoring can thus be done against:

- work actually done (end products produced and tasks completed);

- time taken to date, allocated to each task;

- estimates of the time needed to complete the tasks currently in prog-ress.

Estimates of time to complete tasks should be in man days. Experience has shown that less thought tends to be given to estimates by percentage.

Estimates of time to complete the system must be subject to careful review by senior management as represented in the project board. It must always have the option to suspend, abandon or significantly change the development in the event of unacceptable growth in the estimates.

Regular checkpoint returns from team members should be as simple as possible whilst providing the information needed by the project manager. There should be no need to report data that is available from other sources, or to report the same thing more than once.

CHANGE CONTROL

Changes may be at the request of users or initiated by the developers. Where a proposed change arises from within the Data Processing Department, the proposal must, of course, be agreed by the users.

Changes will usually affect budgets. They may:

- affect work still to be done, which will have a future cost, but will not entail any rework;

- cause rework of items already completed, which can have a more fundamental effect, depending on what has since been built on the earlier products.

While both types of change have their cost, rework represents a waste. Consideration should be given to the causes of such changes with a view to trying to anticipate or avoid them in future developments.

As with every other element of the system, the cost/benefit should be considered and the decision taken whether to:

- include it forthwith;

- put it with other change requests, in order of priority;

- shelve it for the present, but keep it under review for possible future implementation. It will be one of the considerations when trying to anticipate change, and the design should be left as open-ended as possible to accommodate the proposal with the minimum of additional cost in the future;

- reject it, although even if it is decided that it will never be implemented, never is a long time. The proposal could be resurrected under different circumstances in the future. It is advisable to treat it in the same way as those that have been shelved.

The notion of a 'freeze date' is seldom workable in practice. Nevertheless it is a good idea to hold all but essential changes and plan to incorporate them in later releases, after the initial implementation. Of course, anything that entails a major design change should be incorporated as soon as possible to minimise reworking.

The responsibility of deciding whether to implement a change rests ultimately with the project board, but for practical purposes some levels of decision on change may be delegated, depending on cost and time factors:

- Up to some agreed level of cost and delay, the project manager should be authorised to make the decision. Within this control limit, set by the project board, he should have complete responsibility for managing the project. He must report any possibility of exceeding this budget.

- Above these agreed limits, the decision will be a matter for the project board itself.

Decisions to be made by the organisation are:

- agreed levels for delegation to the various decision makers;

- how changes should be recorded;

- how to rate priorities.

Changes are inevitable during all but the shortest of developments. These are caused by:

- changes in the business environment;

- imposed changes, eg due to legislation;

- changes in the technical environment;

- changes or extensions to user requirements.

One of the problems is that in addition to the disruption caused by the change itself, every change is also likely to extend the development time, and the longer the development time, the more opportunity there is for further changes (a good argument for evolutionary development with short timescales for each increment of the system).

Each proposed change requires:

- specification of the change;

- an estimate of the cost of implementing the change;

- an estimate of the effect on the project and on other projects;

- a consideration of the costs and benefits;

- a consideration of the costs of not implementing the change;

- entry in a Change Control Log or Register;

- authorisation, at the appropriate level, to go ahead.

It may be decided to implement a change in the next release of a system, but to include some preparatory work in the current version.

RESCHEDULING

As development continues, the eventual significance of any divergence between actual progress and estimates becomes more obvious. On a project of any significant size, it would be normal for some rescheduling to be needed in the light of actual experience.

DOCUMENT CONTROL

Throughout an SSADM development, new documents are being created and earlier ones amended. It is easy to lose control of the situation, particularly on projects with many team members. Before starting the work, a control system should be devised so that it will be known how many copies there are of every document, who has them, and what changes are incorporated in each new version.

Every different version should have a unique identifier, and arrangements should be made to cancel or recall earlier versions. Much time can be wasted by people working from out of date documents. They are like time bombs lurking in the project.

STATISTICS

Introduction

Data collected during development work forms the basis for estimating and scheduling. Without statistical data, both:

- the refinement of estimates for on-going work, and

- estimates for future work

can only be based either on guesswork or on someone else's experience.

It is now generally accepted that programmer performance is highly variable, with better programmers comparing with poorer ones on a ratio of 10:1 in productivity. Some suggest that the ratio can be as high as 25:1. Obviously one estimate cannot be correct for both extremes, and there is no reason to think that such disparities apply only to programmers.

Statistics, then, are necessary either for the development of one's own estimating method or to permit the calibration of a commercially available model. But this is not the only use of statistics. For example, it is sometimes suggested that they may be used for comparing the performance of different teams, or assessing the impact of different development methods. However, some experience suggests that this is very difficult to do in practice, as each project is different and results are too difficult to interpret.

Among the aspects to be considered are:

- What data is necessary to permit better estimating?

- Who should provide it?

- When should it be obtained?

- How should it be collected?

In the absence of standards and statistics there is no basis for estimates. If the next project will not be developed in the same way that an earlier one was done, then there is no firm basis for making estimates.

SSADM lends itself admirably to the accumulation of statistical data. Every system is developed in the same way, and past experience will therefore give an excellent indication of likely future performance.

Management considerations

It takes time to collect data and to store, maintain and analyse it. Adequate time must be allowed for this, or either the statistical work or the development work (or both) will be skimped. The outcome will be either a poorer system or unreliable statistics.

Management must:

- consider the potential problems of self-recording of performance;

- see what statistics can be obtained automatically, eg from systems software or specially written routines;

- constantly monitor the indicated results to watch for trends and potential problems;

- find why and where actual performance is differing from estimates.

Classification of statistics

The statistics should be classified or annotated to indicate the environment in which they were collected, eg:

- type of system;

- size and complexity of system;

- size of team;

- experience of people involved;

- strategy, eg incremental development, prototyping, etc.

Types of statistics

There are many factors that can influence development time and cost. Enthusiasts for the subject should read *Software Engineering Economics* by Boehm (1981). Some fairly high-level statistics are suggested as follows:

- For the activities:

  - times for each task;

  - times for each step;

  - times for each stage;

  - times for each module.

- For the diagrams:

  - number of data stores on Level-1 logical DFD;

  - number of process boxes on Level-1 logical DFD;

  - number of entities on LDS.

- For the system:

  - number of screens;

  - number of files accessed;

  - number of modules;

  - number of lines of procedural code;

  - size of each module;

  - times to design, code and test each module;

  - elapsed time for each module;

  - time for each life cycle phase.

- For management consideration:

  - details of unscheduled interruptions;

  - details of usage of contingency time;

  - amount of management time.

Use of statistics

Once statistics are available it is possible to come up with some rules of thumb to give very rapid initial sizing. For example, it may be found that in one particular installation:

- on average there are 1.8 modules per screen;

- on average a module takes eight days to code and unit test;

- therefore an average screen takes 14 days to code and test;

- programming takes 30 percent of total development time;

- therefore a screen represents 47 days of development work;

- therefore, a 20 screen system will take 940 days of development effort;

- allowing for absences, effective man days are 3.5 per week;

- the work would therefore take one (average) person 940/3.5 = 269 weeks.

This is not very sophisticated, but does give an early indication of likely time and cost. To provide a closer estimate of elapsed time it will be necessary to consider the non-average people who will be doing the work, how many of them will be available, what work can be done in parallel, and the relevance of the environment in which the statistics were collected (*see Classification of Statistics* on page 139. The comments of Fred Brooks in *The Mythical Man-Month*, that time is not divisible by the number of people available, should always be borne in mind. Projects have a basic time that cannot be reduced. The classic example is: If it will take one woman nine months to have a baby, how long will it take nine women?

22

CASE – Computer Aided Software Engineering

INTRODUCTION

SSADM is a method. Its application is a matter for individual organisations. It can be totally paper based, or it can be supported by software tools.

If the total paper option is chosen, and if the system is of any complexity, then:

- a lot of paper will be generated;

- the cross-checking and cross-referencing will represent a significant workload, and there will inevitably be omissions and mistakes;

Tools which can help and which may already be held include:

- word processors for all documentation and data dictionaries;

- spreadsheets for estimation and control;

- presentation graphics for diagrams;

- a database for holding data extracted from the diagrams.

While all these provide limited help in specific areas of the work, the initial thought required in deciding how best to use them for system development, and the probable lack of integration between them, are severe limitations on their real usefulness.

Case tools are intended to get around these problems and provide an effective development environment.

SUPPORT FOR SSADM

In considering the use of software support, the following points should be established about products under consideration:

- Which version of SSADM do they support?

- What levels of support do they provide for:

  - diagramming?

  - data dictionary?

  - checking within diagrams?

  - cross-checking between diagrams?

  - generation of SSADM forms on screen?

  - enforcement of the method?

- On the diagrams, do they provide all the necessary notation? The following questions may be asked:

  - On DFDs:

    - Do the diagrams allow physical resource flows and resource stores?

    - Do they permit all the alphabetic prefixes to data store numbers, ie D, M, T, T(M)?

    - Can duplication indicators be entered in data stores and external entities?

    - Do they carry data flows forward, complete with notation, to lower level diagrams?

    - Do they permit the decomposition of data flows and data stores on lower level diagrams?

    - Can the lowest level of decomposition indicators be shown in process boxes?

    - Do they permit linkage of external entities?

    - Can system boundaries be drawn on them?

— On the LDS:

- Do they support all the relationships that appear to be true in the early stages of analysis, ie one-to-one, one-to-many, many-to-many? (Whilst all relationships may ultimately resolve into one-to-many, analysts may wish to do this resolution later).

- Do they support multiple, optional, exclusive and recursive relationships?

- Can link phrases be entered?

- Can entities be inserted between other entities to break the relationship lines that are already shown?

- Can notes be added, eg with volumetric information?

— On ELHs:

- Can parallel structures, quits and resumes, state indicators, subsidiary state indicators, operations and the operations list be entered?

- Can ELHs be created for entities before they have been included in the LDS structure?.

— Do they support the other diagrams used in SSADM that is:

- Context Diagram.

- Data Store/Entity Cross-reference.

- Dialogue Structure.

- Document Flow Diagram.

- Effect Correspondence Diagram.

- Enquiry Access Path.

- Enquiry Process Model.

- Input/Output (I/O) Structure Diagram.

- Logical Enquiry Process Model.

- Menu Structure.

- Process Data Interface.

- Process Structure.

- Product Breakdown Structure.

- Product Flow Diagram.

- Prototype Pathway.

- RDBMS (Relational Data Base Management System) Design.

- Resource Flow Diagram.

- Update Process Model.

- If symbols are moved, do all the connecting lines follow them around, or do they have to be redrawn?

- Can symbols be customised to ones more familiar to users?

- Are they single or multi-user? For multi-user systems, what facilities and restrictions are there for several people wanting to work on or view the same diagram at the same time?

- What are the capacities of the tools, ie will they cope with the sizes of systems that are envisaged, in terms of number of entities, processes and stores on DFDs, and levels of DFDs?

- Do they support normalisation of data?

- Do they provide any support for development activities that are not a part of SSADM, for example:

  - strategic study;

  - prioritised selection of systems to be developed;

  - database design;

  - application development.

- For documentation:

  - What output devices are needed for text and for diagrams?

  - How long does it take to produce a typical diagram?

  - If a diagram requires more than one piece of paper, what aids are there to assembling the complete diagram?

- Do they have any accreditation from the SSADM Tool Conformance Scheme run by Birmingham Polytechnic, and if so, at what level?

- Do they support prototyping at any level, for example:

  • screen painting?

  • limited processing?

- Can they support the development of more than one system at the same time (ie will they hold more than one system database)?

GENERAL FEATURES

The points already covered are, of course, additional to the general considerations about *any* software package, for example:

- What does it cost?

- For how long has it been commercially available?

- How many users of the tool are there?

- What security is provided to prevent unauthorised people from gaining access to the system?

- What backup facilities do they provide?

- What is its current version number?

- Can names and addresses of users, ideally in the same business area, be provided for reference purposes?

- What additional charges are there for:

  • maintenance?

  • upgrades?

  • hot line support?

- At what times is hot line support available? (It is worth trying to contact a supplier's hot line number to see how accessible it is. Some seem to be rarely answered, some seem permanently engaged, some will put you on indefinite hold, some promise to phone back and don't. Other users of the tool may well have relevant comments.)

- What hardware and software environments does it require?

- Can colours be customised by users, to help those who are colour blind?

- Are demonstration or evaluation copies available?

- How good is the documentation?

- What training is available from the supplier, and is it part of the package, or a chargeable extra?

- Will it integrate with other software currently in use or likely to be purchased?

- Are any required facilities promised in the future rather than available now? Delays may occur, and priorities for the developers may change.

CONTRACTUAL FEATURES

- Does the right exist to reject the software if it fails user specified acceptance tests?

- What guarantees are there against defects in the package, and for what period?

- Will any verbal claims and promises made by sales people be written into the standard contract?

- What are the costs for purchase/licence to run?

- What discounts are available for use at multiple sites, on more than one computer at the same site, or over networks?

- In the event of the supplier going out of business, what arrangements are there for access to the source code, for example is a copy of the source code lodged with an Escrow Agent? If so, what use would it be?

- What are the maintenance/support costs and arrangements for corrections, upgrades and new releases?

- If customisation of the package is available from the supplier, what is the basis for charges, and how many staff are available for such changes?

- What arrangements can be made for future changes that may be required by the user?

- Is there a charge for hot line support?

SUPPLIER INFORMATION

- What is the reputation of the supplier, for example::

  - For how long has it been in business?

  - What organisations have used its services in the past?

- Does the supplier have a range of packages covering related topics, ie is it an area in which it specialises?

- Did the supplier write the software, or is it acting as an agent?

- Where is the software originator's office, for example, local, UK, Europe, America?

WILL CASE WORK FOR YOU?

Perhaps the most important considerations are those relating to the way in which an analyst works. If the tool will provide a framework on which the facts can be recorded as they are discovered, the work of the analyst will be simplified and paper products kept to a minimum.

Questions to be answered include:

- Does the method of working support the way the work proceeds in practice? The tool may force the analyst to work in the sequence set out in SSADM. This is a logical sequence, but is not the only possible one. Information is not always picked up in a totally logical way in practice. In the earlier stages of analysis, information may be found that SSADM does not require until later. What does the analyst do with information proper to an ELH if he finds it before Step 360? Keeping it on paper until the tool will allow it to be entered is both inefficient and annoying.

- Does the tool enforce checks with other data that the analyst knows to be incomplete, and then refuse to accept it into the system, or can cross checking be invoked when the analyst is ready for it to be done?

Several instances have been reported recently of CASE tools, costing many thousands of pounds, being abandoned by organisations who have become disillusioned.

To take on both a new method and a new development tool at the same time, and then to try to use them both on the development of a new system, may be taking on just a little too much. It is perhaps advisable to employ the method first, and to use it on a simple project initially as suggested in the next chapter.

When you are sure that you are happy with the method you can more safely go on to consider a tool. At that stage you will be much better equipped to know what software help you want, and to evaluate the tools on offer.

23
Introducing the method

INTRODUCTION

There are many good reasons for using SSADM, and they are considered in detail in Chapter 3. However, taking SSADM on board is a major step for any organisation. The effects are far-reaching. The work pattern will change for all those involved, some of whom may never have taken an active part in system development activities before.

Those affected include:

- corporate management;

- user management;

- users;

- computer department management;

- computer systems development staff.

It follows that using SSADM is a course of action that is not to be taken lightly. It requires the commitment of all concerned if systems to be developed using SSADM are to realise their potential in practice.

CORPORATE MANAGEMENT

The effect on corporate management of using SSADM depends on how it views its own responsibilities within the organisation. As computerisation is an avid consumer of resources, then total lack of involvement in system development is an abdication of responsibility.

It is a duty of higher levels of management to ensure that work within the organisation is carried out in an efficient and effective manner. With this aim in mind, senior management involvement should initially be at the strategic level to ensure that:

- the right systems are computerised;

- they are taken on in the best sequence.

The development of a corporate IT strategy lies outside the scope of this book. However, techniques provided by SSADM can be used to help in the development of a strategic plan.

Subsequently, during system development, involvement is needed to ensure that:

- the best methods are being used;

- project management control has been installed;

- QA procedures have been defined and implemented;

- the emerging systems are meeting corporate objectives

Organisations tend to get the computer systems they deserve. If development is left to the technical people, then technically oriented systems are likely to emerge. Systems are much more likely to meet corporate and user objectives if their development is overseen by corporate and user representatives. Projects should have senior managers as sponsors. The sponsors should be represented on, or delegate authority to, a project board.

THE PROJECT BOARD

Representation

Membership of the board should comprise people with sufficient responsibility to take high-level decisions based on what has been done, and to decide whether further work should be carried out. Consequently they are people at senior management or board level who are financially and politically responsible for the project.

Representation on the board is a matter for the organisation and will depend on the project. The SSADM Manual suggests the composition of the board as:

- Executive representation to ensure that corporate interests are always considered

- User department representation to ensure that the emerging system meets the needs of the department. Where the work involves more than one department it may be advisable to extend the user representation accordingly. (Some organisations consider it advisable to have the user who is sponsoring the system as chairman.)

- Computer department or information technology department representation. This is to cover the technical aspects and the availability of resources for the project.

Finance department representation should also be considered to monitor progress against the planned budget, and to see that the projected returns on the capital investment remain within acceptable limits.

For a sufficiently important project, further independent corporate representation may be deemed to be advisable. In all circumstances, this senior project management group should be as small as possible commensurate with the decisions that must be made. Three to five people is probably ideal. A single person would have no formal forum in which to discuss ideas and recommendations. More than five would be in danger of being counter-productive.

It is possible that some smaller projects (or smaller organisations) may choose to have fewer people controlling a project. In this case the responsibilities will remain the same, but they will be represented by fewer people.

Corporate interests should always be the concern of all those who attend, regardless of the size of the board.

Responsibilities

In addition to their parochial concerns, the board members will also have overall authority for ensuring that the project (sometimes more than one project) is under control, ie:

- that the development work completed has not diverged from what was authorised;

- that the project is staying within the agreed constraints of time and cost;

- that there are no significant changes to the cost/benefit ratio;

- to ensure that the project is redirected if external factors (eg changed needs) render the current project deliverables to be out of date (redirection should be carried out only if absolutely essential as it will add to time and cost);

- to decide whether further development should take place;

- to authorise the detailed plans for the next stage of the work, paying particular attention to any significant divergence from estimates made earlier. Each organisation will have to decide what *significant* means, for example 10 percent from budget

Authorisation to continue the project

Continuance to the next development module is based on the detailed plans that have been submitted for approval. This is a critical responsibility. It is never easy to kill a project when a great deal of money has already been spent. Sometimes it must be done in the best interests of the company. The senior managers must not let work continue unless confident of the success of the project, by whatever criteria success will be measured. They must have the authority to do this.

Selection of options

Computer options are considered during the Feasibility Study, during Requirements Analysis when Business Options are presented, and during Logical System Specification when Technical Options are put forward. How the selection is done will vary from organisation to organisation. It will be mainly dependent on the constitution of the QA review team and the project board (and any other committee that the organisation may deem necessary for adequate control to be maintained).

The principles of selection should be seen as funnelling down from the informal range of possibilities put forward initially, to the three (or whatever) for formal selection. This is followed by detailed work on the chosen option. The detail is subject to a formal QA Review. The agreed detailed proposals should then go to the project board for final selection. If the earlier work has been done thoroughly and in full knowledge of corporate objectives, then the project board may have little need to do more than rubber stamp it, with some hybrid option always being a strong possibility.

Any major change deemed necessary at project board level would be likely to result in the discarding of detailed work already done, with its attendant cost. Consequently, proposals going to the project board should always be based on realism, not optimism.

USER MANAGEMENT AND USERS

User management must have a clear understanding of both corporate and system objectives and must be strongly represented in the project management.

Systems must be developed for users. The most important point to understand and accept, for all those involved in a development, is that systems belong to their users. All major decisions must be made by the users, rather than their merely taking part in the decision making. When systems fail to succeed as well as they should, it may be because users:

- will not co-operate;

- do not know how to co-operate;

- are not given the chance to co-operate;

- are not asked the right questions;

- do not know precisely what they want;

- are insufficiently aware of the capabilities of computer technology.

SSADM is designed to involve users from the start of systems analysis. So users are involved in:

- supplying information about what they do (the current system);

- thinking about what can be improved (problems);

- specifying what the new system is to do (requirements);

- specifying in measurable terms how well the new system is to perform (quality objectives);

- specifying in measurable terms the time and cost limits on development and operation of the new system (resource objectives);

- ensuring that their requirements are met (informally by their involvement with the checking and preparation of diagrams, and formally by their participation in quality assurance).

It is a responsibility of user management to ensure that both they and their staff:

- are agreed on the project objectives;

- co-operate in developing a project plan;

- agree user involvement as specified in the plan;

- ensure that their people are available when required;

- take part in informal checking as work progresses;

- know what is expected of them during development;

- understand what is given to them for discussion and QA;

- take part in the formal quality assurance procedures.

This involvement in the analysis, decision making and quality checking processes will take up more of a user's time than the 'traditional' approach. User management must be made aware of the need for this commitment in sufficient time to permit the allocation of resources.

COMPUTER DEPARTMENT MANAGEMENT

Development is changed by the use of SSADM:

- analysis and design are likely to take longer, with savings in all subsequent phases;

- documentation is likely to be more extensive and to require more control.

It is the responsibility of computer department management to:

- ensure that these changes are brought into use with the minimum of disruption and opposition;

- ensure that both the analysts and the users are adequately trained at the right time;

- understand the change in work pattern and hence in the deployment of resources;

- install a project control system to take advantage of the estimation and control facilities that become available with SSADM;

- consider the use of software tools to reduce development effort and to automate the routine checks between documents.

Computer department management should be represented on the project board.

THE PROJECT MANAGER

The day-to-day control of a project is the responsibility of a project manager.

Basic skills

As the job title implies, the task requires management skills. Besides these, the manager must also:

- be experienced in project management techniques;

- have an adequate knowledge of SSADM;

- have experienced advice available to him.

The management resource

It is essential that the project manager should be allocated sufficient time to manage the project effectively.

In a small project, the team leader will normally be the manager. He may also be responsible for some of the key elements of the work that require experience beyond that of the other team members.

A larger project, with more than one project team, will need a management structure. In this case the manager may well be fully occupied with management activities. More detailed involvement with the technical work is likely to have a detrimental effect on the control activities and hence on cost and delivery date.

Background experience

Given the basic skills mentioned above, the project manager need not necessarily be a technical expert in systems development. A user who has adequate training can effectively manage the Feasibility Study and Requirements Analysis Modules. A user manager will also be able to resolve many of the queries that arise, that would otherwise require a more time-consuming expedition to the user department.

Change of manager

The same project manager may control a project through Feasibility Study to implementation, and this is usually the most effective way. However, it is not always possible for the same person to carry a project all the way through, and different skills and techniques are needed at different stages of development. Other alternatives, if it is not possible to have the same manager throughout, or it is deemed preferable to change, are:

- different managers for:

  • systems analysis;

  • systems design;

- program design, construction and implementation;

- different managers for:

- SSADM activities;

- subsequent activities.

THE TEAM LEADER

For a small project, the team leader may also be the project manager.

The team leader needs to have:

- training in and experience of team leadership;

- an expert knowledge of SSADM;

- the basic analysis and design skills.

Regardless of the nature of the role (team leader or manager), adequate time must be scheduled for the role activities. Otherwise some element of the work — managerial or technical — will suffer.

The responsibilities of the team leader include:

- activity control;

- change control;

- informal QA Reviews to maintain a detailed view of the products of the team;

- formal QA Reviews.

PROJECT TEAMS

Introduction

In *The Psychology of Computer Programming* Weinberg suggests that the basic rule for size and composition of programming teams for the best programming at the least cost is to:

"...give the best possible programmers you can find sufficient time so you need the smallest number of them. When you have to work faster, or with less experienced people, costs and uncertainties will rise. In any case, the worst way to do a programming project is to hire a horde of trainees and put them to work under pressure and without supervision..."

Whilst Weinberg was referring specifically to programmers, the same findings apply to all development staff. This is a topic that is discussed very readably by Brooks in *The Mythical Man-Month* — a book that should come high on any compulsory reading list.

TEAM STRUCTURE

Experience has shown that the ideal team structure for an SSADM development is as shown in Figure 23.1.

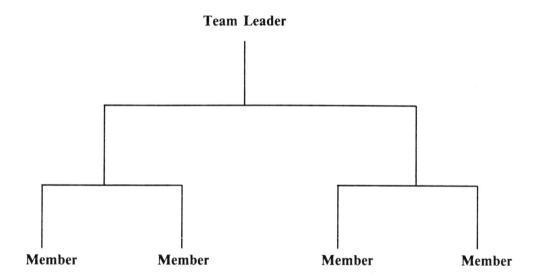

Figure 23.1 An SSADM team structure

This gives a team organisation capable of dealing with the three main types of work that occur under SSADM, ie:

- work which can be done individually, eg Relational Data Analysis (Step 340) and the preparation of Update and Enquiry Process Models (Steps 520 and 530);

- work best done in pairs; this applies mainly to the diagramming techniques, and particularly to DFDs and ELHs;

- team work, eg brainstorming sessions when options are being created.

However, such an organisation is not always possible, and many projects are developed with fewer people.

Multiple project teams

Where work is beyond the capacity of a single small team, the requisite number of people can be built up from teams of five to give a structure of the kind depicted in Figure 23.2.

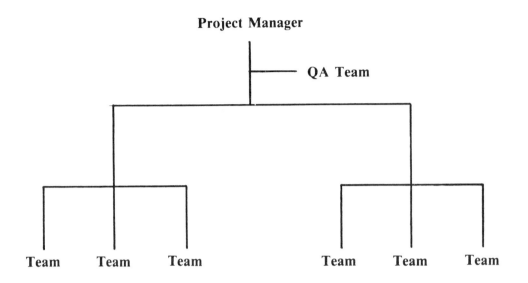

Figure 23.2 An SSADM team structure for a larger project

This is, of course, only one of many possible structures, but the small team concept should not be discarded lightly. It has much to offer, both in efficiency and effectiveness.

Work should be allocated to teams by business functional area, and not by SSADM tasks or techniques. The techniques gain their strength from their interaction with each other. To have them done in isolation is likely to give poorer individual products and more problems when they are brought together.

The products of the separate teams must be co-ordinated as the work proceeds. This may be the responsibility of the manager (or an intermediate level of management if project size requires layers of management). It could also be the responsibility of one of the teams, perhaps with other specialist roles, for example:

- monitoring standards;

- organising the QA Reviews (but not carrying them out);

- providing expert assistance on SSADM.

INTRODUCING SSADM INTO AN ORGANISATION

Obtain corporate approval and commitment

The introduction of SSADM will cost money both in terms of the direct expenditure and the fact that computer staff will not be able to carry out other duties because of the need for training. There may be further expenses on consultants and on CASE software.

It will involve many people at all levels in the company. Senior management must be aware of the changes that will occur, be prepared for the costs, and be committed to its use. This applies particularly to ensuring co-operation from users and understanding that time will be lost in their normal work as a consequence.

SSADM will need corporate approval and commitment if it is to succeed.

Choose a pilot project

Projects which an organisation may wish to develop, possibly as a result of a detailed strategic analysis, should be considered with a view to selecting a project that would be suitable for pilot use of the method.

The characteristics of a project suitable for a pilot study should include some of the following:

- scheduled to start in a few weeks, to allow adequate time to organise suitable training;

- short in duration, for example, capable of development by a small team with analysis and design measured in weeks rather than months, and with an elapsed time of no more than six to nine months with the resources that will be available;

- non-critical to the continued existence of the company;

- non-urgent, perhaps by bringing forward a project that had been scheduled for later development;

- requiring no technical experience beyond that already held by the development team;

- in a business area that is already familiar to the analysts;

- not requiring any pioneering work and not likely to need major hardware purchases;

- considered to be fairly restricted in its corporate impact, ie only one or two user departments will be involved;

- with user involvement readily available.

In other words, there should be no pressure, and the only new element in the development should be SSADM itself.

Maybe there really is no alternative other than to start with a development that is big, complex or innovatory. In those circumstances every effort should be made to identify a distinct part of the total system that would be suitable as the pilot. If this is not possible, then consideration should be given to obtaining the services of someone who is already an expert in the use of the method.

Choose a project team

Try to choose a team leader who is keen to use SSADM, and who is also credible in the eyes of the rest of the team and the installation. As SSADM skills are much in demand, self interest should ensure that a suitable candidate will not prove too difficult to find. When problems arise, as inevitably they will, an interested and enthusiastic team leader should be able to see them through.

If possible, at least two people should be involved in the pilot project. This permits some discussion and teamwork, provides some cover to a development that would otherwise be very vulnerable to staff absences, and permits practical experience of the method to be made available more quickly around the installation.

Ideally all team members should share the enthusiasm for SSADM, but it would be quite normal to find that at least some of the people felt that their creativity was being stifled, and who considered that standards were like a strait-jacket. There are several points that can be made to them:

- Analysis − the finding of facts − is not an act of creation, it is a task of research. SSADM does not stifle this − it encourages it and provides tools to make it more thorough.

- The areas where creativity always existed are expanded. With the traditional approach, creation tended to be channelled towards a single solution for the design. In SSADM they are expected to propose several different possible choices for a Feasibility Option, more alternatives for a Business System Option, and then several more for the Technical System Option.

- Excellent reasons for using standards are discussed in Chapter 2. Try fitting an old two-pin plug to their electric kettle and see how they feel about standards then.

   — If all reasoning fails, they could perhaps be made to realise that they are
     employed to provide an efficient and effective service for their employers,
     and not for their own private amusement.

Arrange training

Practitioners

Training of the practitioners should not be undertaken until the first project is
ready to start. The ideal situation is for the trainee to come off the course and
make an immediate start on the pilot project. To come off the course and then
do something else for a couple of months really makes no sense at all.

   Most courses offer separate weeks for analysis and for design, running
consecutively. Whilst the weeks may be booked separately, it is preferable to take
them together whenever possible. This is because analysts will be completing
documentation in the first week without appreciating its use in the subsequent
design.

   SSADM courses are not general systems analysis courses. SSADM assumes that
its practitioners will have the basic skills such as interviewing, fact finding,
proposal writing, presentations, form design, screen design, and all the rest.
These skills are needed as much in SSADM as with any other approach. Some
practical experience of analysis and design is highly desirable before starting out
on SSADM.

   Some basic training courses now incorporate the SSADM approach, thus
allowing trainees to make an early contribution within an SSADM environment.

   Public courses may be the best option for training the pilot team members in
SSADM skills. Assuming that their practical experience is satisfactory, then in-
house training may be preferable (and cheaper) for a wider take-on of the
method. An in-house course also gives the opportunity for questions to be raised
about actual systems to be developed within the installation.

Project managers

Project managers are not necessarily involved in the detailed SSADM production
work, but require more knowledge of the method than do the users. They need
to know both the structure of the method and the documentation that will be
produced. The full training course is advisable for them — again as and when
needed. This will be earlier than the team members because of the planning they
must do.

End users

In this context, users include project board members, QA reviewers, those involved in the lower level fact finding and informal reviews, and future users of the system after implementation.

When it comes to computing, users range from the enthusiastic to the fearful. If their previous experience has been to read and sign off a specification that bordered on the incomprehensible (so far as they were concerned), they may well be prepared for the worst. Users are not likely, initially, to be any more taken by the diagramming techniques than they were with blocks of text. This is particularly so if the diagrams are crammed with boxes, and created for reasons of which they have no knowledge.

Users need training every bit as much as the practitioners do, but it must be a different training. They need to appreciate much of what was covered in the first six chapters of this book, ie:

- Why a method is necessary.

- What SSADM has to offer.

- An outline of SSADM.

- The elements of a system.

- The use and purpose of diagrams.

This must then be supplemented with sufficient information about the diagrams to be able to understand them. They have no need to know how to construct the diagrams, or to check that they stick to standards.

Users must also be made aware of their involvement in the development process and what it entails:

- supplying the information that the analysts need;

- specifying their requirements for the system, ie functions, qualities, and resource usage;

- informally checking the diagrams as they are produced;

- formally being involved at QA points;

- selecting the Business System Option;

- selecting the Technical System Option.

Use consultants

A team tackling their first project with the method may have trouble in all sorts of ways, for example, in knowing:

- how to start;

- what level to go to;

- when to stop;

- why they are doing what they are doing;

- how the techniques and products fit together;

- how to customise the method for the particular project in hand (although for the first project it is advisable to omit nothing, and regard it all as part of the learning process).

An experienced consultant can be invaluable in resolving such uncertainties, and keeping the project on the road. This does not mean that he must be present throughout the life of the project. It means having a consultant in for a day or so at strategic times, perhaps:

- within a day or so of the start, to resolve the initial problems;

- a week or so later to check progress made and to put right anything that is going wrong, before too much time is wasted;

- at the end of the first step, to assist with QA on the products that then exist;

- at other QA points.

A useful guide would be to arrange to have the services of a consultant for an average of one day every two weeks, subject to negotiation as to the actual day of visit, perhaps on occasions grouping two or three days together.

It would also be useful to have advice fairly readily available through telephone support.

Define the standards to be used

Most organisations have standards of some sort. Examples are:

- a project control method;

- a quality assurance method;

- a program design method;

- a way of documenting the work;

- a filing system;

- a non-documented but accepted way of doing things.

Unless an existing analysis and design method is being replaced by SSADM, then acquiring SSADM will supplement rather than replace existing standards. It will, however, impact on the existing standards, and the impact must be considered, for example:

- Project control before SSADM may be based on different:

  - estimating methods;

  - checkpoints;

  - documents and procedures.

- Some SSADM documents may be very similar to documents that are already in use in the installation. This may cause modification to either the installation documents or the SSADM documents, or possibly the creation of new documents incorporating features from both.

- A filing system may already be in place. The *Version 3 SSADM Manual, Volume 2,* suggests ways of filing documents for both users and non-users of NCC's *Data Processing Documentation Standards.* A third possibility is the integration of the SSADM documentation within the existing installation documentation system.

It is likely that organisations with existing standards will find some conflict with the standards in SSADM. It is important that the essence of SSADM is not lost, but differences in detail should not be allowed to cause any hang-ups, for example:

- the method may be changed in minor details to fit in with accepted and proven local practice;

- existing practices may be changed to those within SSADM;

- the symbols to be used on the diagrams should be agreed, for example, crows feet, forks or arrowheads on the LDS, numbering of boxes on the DFDs, the shape of the symbols on all the diagrams, how connectors are represented, etc.

Any divergence from SSADM standards should be specified in an introductory document if external resources are to be used for any aspect of development or subsequent maintenance.

Monitor progress

It is worth recording details of the work, for example:

- time taken for each separately identifiable element, ie below task level wherever possible;

- notes of problems encountered;

- anywhere where it has been considered necessary to diverge from or to augment the method;

- system statistics as mentioned in Chapter 21;

- lack of experience in any area of the work, other than the use of the method itself, for example, new business area, Technical Option selected that has not been used before.

Plan ahead

The estimates for future system developments, as featured in the strategic plan, should be reconsidered in the light of experience of the pilot project.

References

Albrecht A J, Gaffney J E, Software function. source lines of code, and development effort predictions: a software science validation, *IEE Transactions on Software Engineering,* Vol SE – 9, No.6, pp 639 – 648, November 1983.

Behrens C A, Measuring the productivity of computer systems development activites with function points, *IEE Transactions on Software Engineering,* Vol SE – 9, No 6, pp 648 – 652, November 1983.

Boehm B, *Software Engineering, IEE Transactions on Computers,* Vol C – 25 December 1976.

Boehm B W, *Software Engineering Economics,* Prentice Hall, 1981.

Brooks F P, *The Mythical Man – Month – Essays on Software Engineering,* Addison – Wesley Publishing Company, 1975.

Fagan M E, *Design and Code Inspections to Reduce Errors in Program Development,* IBM Systems Journal, Vol 15, No 3, 1976.

Gilb T, *Principles of Software Engineering Management,* Addison – Wesley Publishing Company, 1988.

Ingevaldsson L, *JSP – a Practical Method of Program Design,* Chartwell-Bratt, 1980.

Jackson M A, *Principles of Program Design,* Academic Press, 1975.

Longworth, G, Nicholls D P *SSADM Manual,* NCC Publications, 1986.

Longworth G, Nicholls D P, Abbott J, *SSADM Developer's Handbook,* NCC Publications, 1988.

Longworth G, *Getting the System You Want: A User's Guide to SSADM,* NCC Publications, 1989.

Nicholls D P, *Introducing SSADM,* NCC Publications, 1987.

PA Computers and Telecommunications, *Benefits of Software Engineering Methods and Tools: A Study for the Department of Trade and Industry,* Department of Trade and Industry, 1985.

Peters L J *Software Design: Methods and Techniques,* Yourdon Inc, 1981.

Proctor I M, *Project Management and Control Manual,* NCC Publications, 1988.

Putnam L H, Tutorial: *Software Cost – Estimating and Life Cycle Control,* IEEE, 1980.

Weinberg G M, *The Psychology of Computer Programming,* Van Nostrand Reinhold, 1971.

Index